LIVING VICTORIOUSLY IN CHRIST
GROWING IN CHRIST

A 30 Day Devotional

By

Cindy Cross & Lisa Vanderbilt

CROSSLINK PUBLISHING

Living Victoriously in Christ: Growing in Christ

CrossLink Publishing
www.crosslinkpublishing.com

Copyright, © 2013 Cindy Cross & Lisa Vanderbilt

All rights reserved. No part of this book may be reproduced in any form, except for brief quotations in reviews, without the written permission of the author.

Printed in the United States of America. All rights reserved under International Copyright Law.

ISBN 978-1-936746-51-4
Library of Congress Control Number: 2013937687

All scripture quotations, unless otherwise indicated are taken from the Holy Bible, New International Version®, NIV®. Copyright © 1973, 1978, 1984, 2011 by Biblica, Inc.™ Used by permission of Zondervan. All rights reserved worldwide. www.zondervan.com The "NIV" and "New International Version" are trademarks registered in the United States Patent and Trademark Office by Biblica, Inc.™

Scripture quotations marked "KJV" are taken from the King James Version of the Holy Bible.

Scripture quotations marked "ESV" are taken from The Holy Bible, The English Standard Version® (ESV®), copyright © 2001 by Crossway, a publishing ministry of Good News Publishers. Used by permission. All rights reserved.

Scripture quotations marked "NKJV" are taken from The Holy Bible, the New King James Version®. Copyright © 1982 by Thomas Nelson, Inc. Used by permission. All rights reserved.

Scripture quotations marked "The Message" are taken from THE MESSAGE. Copyright © by Eugene H. Peterson 1993, 1994, 1995, 1996, 2000, 2001, 2002. Used by permission of NavPress Publishing Group."

DEDICATION

This book is dedicated first and foremost to God because the vision was His. Each of these daily devotionals was inspired by Him because without His direction, we could have never written them ourselves.

Thanks to our husbands and families for their understanding and patience as we spent time writing this book.

Special thanks goes to our friend, Vanessa Jones, for her godly input into the making of this book.

Special thanks also goes to Senior Pastor Brandon Groome and to the Elders of Southwest Christian Church for allowing us to use the facilities for our weekly meetings.

CONTENTS

DAY 1: I Had To Be In My Father's House 1
DAY 2: No Pain, No Gain - Hope in Your Suffering 5
DAY 3: What Are You Starving For? 9
DAY 4: Just One Second 13
DAY 5: I Know Nothing! 19
DAY 6: Spiritual Invalid 23
DAY 7: To Whom Much Is Given 29
DAY 8: What Does Your Future Hold? 33
DAY 9: The Temple of God 39
DAY 10: It Is Well With My Soul 45
DAY 11: Me, A Priest? 51
DAY 12: A Penny for Your Thoughts 57
DAY 13: How Is Your Foundation? 63
DAY 14: Jack-in-the-Box God 69
DAY 15: Lift Up Your Face 75
DAY 16: "Just" Pray 81
DAY 17: Who's Your Enemy? 85
DAY 18: Expecting God 91
DAY 19: Give Careful Thought 95
DAY 20: Hearing God 101
DAY 21: Through the Pain 107
DAY 22: You Can't Fool God! 111
DAY 23: Soaking Up the Word 117
DAY 24: Out of Control! 123
DAY 25: It's Time to Surrender! 129

DAY 26: Day By Day 135
DAY 27: Basic Instructions for Life 141
DAY 28: Making the Most of Your Time 147
DAY 29: Go Figure 153
DAY 30: Perfection and Excellence 159
APPENDIX A 163
REFERENCES 167
A WORD FROM LVC MINISTRIES 169
ABOUT THE AUTHORS 171

FORWARD

"Living Victoriously is a devotional study offering practical insights on a wide range of helpful biblical subjects. More importantly the authors live victoriously themselves! Cindy and Lisa walk the walk and have tirelessly shared this counsel with their own Christian family. This study will bless and encourage your walk with Christ."

Brandon J. Groome
Senior Minister, Southwest Christian Church
Fort Worth, Texas

"God called Cindy and Lisa to reach out and share with everyone how to live and grow in Christ by getting His message out through this devotional. It has everything you need for day to day living from Bible scriptures, prayers for you to pray, questions to ask yourself and information that makes you stop and think about the love God has for us.

Living Victoriously in Christ shows you, step by step, how to grow in Christ and as you grow in Him you become victorious in Him. Cindy and Lisa have shared their stories with us to encourage and strengthen us in God's Word.

I have found great strength and comfort in this devotional. It has helped me through some very tough times in my life. Living Victoriously in Christ - Growing in Christ will be a blessing to you as it has been for me. I HIGHLY recommend this devotional for everyone!"

Linda Felton
Cabot, Arkansas

"For everyone who has been born of God overcomes the world. And this is the victory that has overcome the world— our faith. Who is it that overcomes the world except the one who believes that Jesus is the Son of God?"
1 John 5:4-5 (ESV)

DAY 1

I Had To Be In My Father's House
By Cindy

"Why were you searching for me?" he asked. "Didn't you know I had to be in my Father's house?"
—Luke 2:49

When Jesus was 12 years old his parents lost track of him when they were all in Jerusalem for the Feast of the Passover. After searching for him for 3 days, they finally found him in the temple. Mary and Joseph were astonished when they found him and wanted to know why he treated them like that. Truth be known, Jesus was probably just as surprised by their actions. He couldn't understand why they were searching for him, since they should have known that he would be in his Father's house or, as the King James Version states, *"I must be about my Father's business."* Luke 2:49.

As Christians, what does that say about us? John 1:12 tells us, *"to all who received him, to those who believed in his name, he gave the right to become children of God"*. As a son or daughter of God, shouldn't we also make it a priority to be about His business? After all, Christ gave His life for you. This week, take some time out of your busy schedule and ask God what business of His He wants you to do.

In Luke 2:49, Jesus makes it sound so simple, yet, it's not simple. It's hard to always be about our Father's business. We get caught up in life. Oh yes, the desire is there, but we are only human . . . and God knows that, because as our Creator, He knows each one of us, personally.

QUESTIONS TO PONDER

1. What is getting in your way of making God's business a priority?

2. What can you remove from your busy schedule in order to do God's business?

3. Is it hard for you to do God's work? Why or why not?

4. God knows each one of us personally. Do you know Him that way?

GOD'S WORD TO YOU

So do not fear, for I am with you; do not be dismayed, for I am your God. I will strengthen you and help you; I will uphold you with my righteous right hand.
Isaiah 41:10

DAILY PRAYER

Dear Father,
My prayer to You today is that my eyes and my heart be opened to You! Give me the desire to keep You in the center of my life so that I can stay grounded and focused on what really matters. Lord, gently remind me that when I am running from one thing to the next, that my eyes are not on You. Give me the desire to be in Your house and to be about Your business, because it is Your mercy and grace that allow me to have the things I have and all blessings given to me, flow directly from You. I ask this in the name of your precious Son, Jesus Christ! Amen.

DAY 2

No Pain, No Gain - Hope in Your Suffering
By Lisa

Have you ever started a new workout plan? As you begin, and your muscles ache from the new workout regimen, I bet you were thinking, "No pain, no gain!" But is that true for our spiritual lives? Do you have to have pain to grow spiritually? I suppose you don't *have* to have pain to grow, but the pain and suffering that we go through *will* help us to grow exponentially if we allow it to. I know that for *me personally*, I have grown more spiritually during times of pain and suffering than at any other time. I suspect many of you would say the same thing. It's during those times that we really bear down and rely on God. Most of us have noticed that when we're not suffering, we can get comfortable and complacent, and we find that we don't want to change. We like the feeling that we have control of our lives. Then something unexpected happens, forcing us to change. Change itself can cause pain and suffering. What is it that's forcing you to change? A death? A divorce? An illness? A betrayal? The loss of a job? The list is endless. But there is hope! We gain perseverance, character, and hope through our suffering. Romans 5:3-4 says that *"...we also rejoice in our sufferings, because we know that suffering produces perseverance; perseverance, character; and character, hope."* You may wonder, "How can a person rejoice in their suffering?" Take a look at how you have grown in your character as you look to God in your trials. Your growth in these times is a reason to be joyful. And you can have hope that one day it will all be over, whether here on earth, or in eternity with Jesus. As you trust in Jesus, you can know that you are able to do all things through Him who gives you strength. (Philippians 4:13) You *can't* do it on your own, but you *can* make it through this time as you lean on Him. And as you do, He will give you His joy and a peace that surpasses understanding while you are in the midst of your trials. (Phl 4:7) God does not promise that there will be no suffering, but that *in* your suffering, He will be with you. He will never leave you. Don't let your suffering go to waste. Use it to persevere and to grow your character. Work your spiritual muscles and your faith will increase as you see God at work in your life.

QUESTIONS TO PONDER

1. How do you find comfort during painful times?

2. In what ways can you work your spiritual muscles?

3. Do you find that you are only going to God in times of suffering? What do you need to do to change that?

4. How have you grown through past or present pain?

5. Do you personally rejoice in your suffering? How can you do this?

GOD'S WORD TO YOU

Be imitators of God, therefore, as dearly loved children and live a life of love, just as Christ loved us and gave himself up for us as a fragrant offering and sacrifice to God.
Ephesians 5:1-2

DAILY PRAYER

Heavenly Father,
As I go through suffering and pain, I ask that You would give me Your joy and Your peace through trying times. Help me to see the hope that You offer. Thank You for growing me spiritually and giving me the strength to go through these tough times, not alone, but with You. And thank You for increasing my faith as I trust in You. In Jesus name I pray. Amen.

DAY 3

What Are You Starving For?
By Cindy

Everyone is starving for something. Some people are starving for power, love, money, attention, and materialistic things....What are you starving for? As Christians we should be starving for God, hungering for His Word and His presence within us. There are many lost people out there in the world that are starving for what we have; their soul is hungry for salvation. It's interesting, we have what they want, what they are desperately searching for, but we hang on to it like we are the privileged few.

I tell people that I feel like I was born in church; my parents had me there every time the doors opened. Even after I got married, if I missed a service, I felt like I had a hundred parents asking me, "Where were you Sunday?" In 1984, my husband and I moved to Florida and we got into the worldly mindset, "Well, I worked all week, and all day in the yard on Saturday, so I'm going to sleep late on Sunday." Needless, to say, we got out of church, and stayed out for 18 years! When we had an opportunity to transfer to Texas in 2002, God said, *"You've been starving long enough. It's time to come back to me!"*

Since that time, God has steadily been working in me, to get me where I am at this moment. During quiet time the other day, I was flipping through my Bible and saw this passage that I had highlighted and marked with an asterisk: *"Restore to me the joy of Your salvation and grant me a willing spirit, to sustain me. Then I will teach transgressors Your ways, and sinners will turn back to You."* Psalm 51:12-13. As I read this passage again, I remembered how hungry I was for God at the time and the fact that I highlighted it with an asterisk meant that I desperately wanted it. I realize now that God is blessing me because He is fulfilling these verses in my life today. He has restored the joy of His salvation to me and I am at peace. His desire is my desire—to help starving Christians get filled to their potential and to lead sinners to Christ.

As a Christian, if you are starving for a closer walk with Christ, then continuously ask Him to restore in you the joy of His salvation. Pray to Him unceasingly; study His Word to see what it is that He has to say to you, and then ask Him to use you. His greatest desire is that everyone comes to Him, so don't be surprised if He sends someone to you who *is* starving, someone whose soul is hungry for salvation.

QUESTIONS TO PONDER

1. *Everyone is starving for something. What are you starving for?*

2. *What are you filling your heart and mind with?*

3. *In what ways are you seeking a closer relationship with God?*

4. *Is it a struggle for you to go to church or for you to read your Bible? If so, why?*

GOD'S WORD TO YOU

Create in me a pure heart, O God, and renew a steadfast spirit within me.
Psalm 51:10

DAILY PRAYER

Dear Father,
I ask You to renew in me the joy of Your salvation and give me a hunger for You, for Your Word and for those who are lost because I know that the empty space that they are trying to fill in their souls is a God sized hole that can only be filled by You. Because of Your mercy and grace and the sacrifice of Your Son, Jesus, You have given me the way and means to find solace and that peace comes only through direct communion with You. I ask this in the name of your Son, Jesus Christ! Amen.

DAY 4

Just One Second
By Cindy

I was listening to a CD the other day and heard the song, *"Give Me Your Eyes"*[1] by Brandon Heath. In it Brandon sings, *"Give me Your eyes for just one second. Give me Your eyes so I can see everything that I keep missing, give me Your love for humanity. Give me Your arms for the brokenhearted. Give me Your heart for the one's forgotten."*[2]

I was thinking, what if God did give us His eyes for just one second? Would we be able to handle it? *Could* we handle it? Do we truly want this or do we just say that we do? I had one such incident happen to me several years ago. As I was walking into a grocery store, a lady was walking toward me and being a typical female, I thought to myself, *"What is that outfit she is wearing?"* Then of course, I felt bad for thinking that and I whispered a prayer to God, *"Lord, just let me see her as you see her!"* When I turned around to look at her, I felt a feeling of total love! I actually wanted to chase after the woman and tell her that I loved her!

I've thought of that incident many, many times since and I've never forgotten the feeling of overwhelming, total love! When I asked God to let me see her as He sees her, I really didn't expect to get a response and I certainly wasn't expecting a feeling of such *complete* love. God showed me that day that He is not concerned with what a person is wearing. He's not concerned with our social status and He's certainly not concerned with our race . . . . So I'm wondering now, why *are we concerned* with all that stuff? What would happen if each one of us asked God to open our eyes, for just one second, and let us see humanity as He sees it?

I don't know why God let me see that lady through His eyes and to feel the overwhelming love for her that He had for her, but, I do know that it was a humbling experience. I also know that the love I felt was not even close to the full measure of love that God feels because He knew that I would not have been able to handle it! God is constantly molding us and shaping us to become like Christ. Ephesians 4:24 tells us to *" . . . put on the new self, created to be like God in true righteousness and holiness."*

Everywhere you look there are lost people, people who need to know Jesus Christ as their personal Savior. We do have a heart for lost people and like Jesus we don't want to see anyone spend eternity separated from the love of God. But, we really can't completely work for God unless we see with His eyes, and feel with His heart the total love that He has for everyone. To get to that point, we have to be obedient, working for God and surrendering ourselves to His total will.

This week as you go about your business, ask God to give you His eyes so that you might see everything that you have been missing. Ask God to give you His arms for the broken hearted so that you can reach out to them. Ask God to give you His heart for the ones who are forgotten. Ask God to give you His love for humanity. A*sk God to give you His eyes for just one second!*

QUESTIONS TO PONDER

1. Have you ever asked God to give you His eyes? Why or why not?

2. If God did give you His eyes, even for one second, what do you think you would see?

3. God loves every person unconditionally and equally. Why do you think that we differentiate between people?

4. In your own words, how do you think God sees you?

5. How do you see people?

GOD'S WORD TO YOU

*Turn my eyes away from worthless things;
preserve my life according to your word.*
Psalm 119:37

DAILY PRAYER

*Dear Father God,
You see so much more than I could possibly ever imagine! There are so many people in my circle that I meet or pass each day that are lonely, hurting and desperately need to know Jesus Christ as his or her personal Savior. Father, if it is Your will, give me Your eyes so that I might see where I can work for You. Show me the broken hearted, the lonely, hurting people and please, Lord, give me Your love for all of humanity! Use me, Father, to do Your perfect and everlasting will. In the name of Jesus Christ I pray! Amen.*

DAY 5

I Know Nothing!
By Lisa

Remember the old sitcom, "Hogan's Heroes"?[3] Colonel Hogan and his crew, who ran a special operations group from within the Stalag 13 POW camp, were always pulling one over on Colonel Klink. Whenever Sergeant Schultz would find that Colonel Hogan was up to something, he would turn a blind eye and say, "I know nothing! I know nothing!" (Remember, you have to say it with a German accent!)

It made me think about how often we claim, "I know nothing!" about God's Word and His truths. Sometimes it seems easier if we don't know something, because then we think we're not responsible. We believe that "ignorance is bliss." But when it comes to God's Word, ignorance is not bliss. We are accountable to know what's in God's Word. God expects us to read His Word and obey what it says. And when we do, we'll have rewards and blessings in this life and the one to come. Knowing Jesus is what brings blessings, or bliss, to our lives. God doesn't want us to obey Him because we are afraid of Him, He wants us to obey Him because we love Him. To know Jesus and to have a personal relationship with Him is what life is truly all about. When we know who Jesus is and that He died for our sins on the cross so that we can have eternal life, then we find that we love Him because of His love for us. The bible tells us, *"We love because He first loved us."* (1 John 4:19) And when you love Him and believe what He did and who He is, the bible and its truths will open up to you in a special way – They will come alive to you, and you will want to be obedient to God.

If you're going to be ignorant about anything, it should be about the world. What I mean by that is that we should have the philosophy that Paul had. In 1 Corinthians 2:2, Paul said, *"For I resolved to know nothing while I was with you except Jesus Christ and him crucified."* Paul's focus was on Jesus. If anything, he was putting aside everything *except* God's Word and his relationship with Jesus. He was focusing totally on Jesus. So let's bring this home for us. How can you bring Jesus more fully into your life? Have you asked Him to reveal Himself to you? Are you continuing in His Word daily? Do you believe that His Word is the truth? Do you pray to Him and listen to what He has to say to you? These things will help you to draw closer to Him. And then you won't want to be ignorant and know nothing. You'll be soaking up everything you can from God and His Word, because it's not ignorance that's bliss, it's "knowing" Him that is bliss.

QUESTIONS TO PONDER

1. How do you get to know God?

2. Do you obey God because you love Him or because you're afraid of Him?

3. How has God revealed Himself to you?

4. Where is your focus?

5. Is ignorance bliss, or is "knowing" bliss?

GOD'S WORD TO YOU

If you remain in me and my words remain in you, ask whatever you wish, and it will be given you.
John 15:7

DAILY PRAYER

Dear Heavenly Father,
Thank You for the truth of Your Word. Father, I ask that You would draw me closer to You. Teach me from Your Word. Show me what I need to do to focus on Jesus throughout my days. And then show me how I need to change to be obedient to You. Thank You for loving me and revealing Yourself to me. In Jesus name I pray. Amen.

DAY 6

Spiritual Invalid
By Lisa

"Some time later, Jesus went up to Jerusalem for a feast of the Jews. ^{2}Now there is in Jerusalem near the Sheep Gate a pool, which in Aramaic is called Bethesda and which is surrounded by five covered colonnades. ^{3}Here a great number of disabled people used to lie—the blind, the lame, the paralyzed. ^{5}One who was there had been an invalid for thirty-eight years. ^{6}When Jesus saw him lying there and learned that he had been in this condition for a long time, he asked him, "Do you want to get well?" ^{7}"Sir," the invalid replied, "I have no one to help me into the pool when the water is stirred. While I am trying to get in, someone else goes down ahead of me." ^{8}Then Jesus said to him, "Get up! Pick up your mat and walk." ^{9}At once the man was cured; he picked up his mat and walked."

—John 5:1-9

This story of the healing of the invalid really hits home for me. I was never an invalid physically, but I was one spiritually for many years – almost as many years as the invalid in this story. For many of my first 36 years I went to church and sat on the pews. I was spoon-fed the Word of God as a baby would be spoon-fed his milk. My nourishment of spiritual milk came mostly on Sundays and occasionally on Wednesdays, which made me very weak spiritually. I even stopped going to church altogether for a number of years, so my spiritual malnourishment continued to worsen. I was like those disabled people at Bethesda. I was spiritually blind, lame and paralyzed. I had accepted Christ as a child, but I was blind to who He truly was, and who I was in Him. I was like the lame man in this story who couldn't move into the pool. I had no idea how bad my spiritual situation was. I was spiritually paralyzed and not able to move forward with the plans God had for me.

Then Jesus began to speak to me in a way I had never heard Him before. In essence, He asked me if I wanted to get well. He changed my desires into His desires. Previously, there were times that I felt very much alone, like the invalid who had no one to put him into the pool. But with Jesus there, I had all the help I needed. And the truth of it was, I did have others around who cared about me and were praying for me. The problem is that I was so focused on myself that I felt all alone. But Jesus finally helped me to focus my attention on Him. He fed me meat from the Word, giving me spiritual strength. And when He told me to get up and walk, I was able to do it in the strength that *He* gave me. Now I help feed others spiritually by writing and speaking the Word of God. And if there is hope for me, there is certainly hope for you!

Do you feel like a spiritual invalid? Do you feel like you are blind, lame or paralyzed? The question for you is the one Jesus asks all of us in that condition… *"Do you want to get well?"* If so, I believe Jesus would tell you the same thing… *"Get up! Pick up your mat and walk!"* Walk in the life that Jesus has for you! Stop dwelling where you are and choose to be healed spiritually. Is God asking you to do something that is a bit challenging that you've been putting off? Those challenging situations will help you grow spiritually as the Holy Spirit guides you. No longer must you choose the life of the blind, lame or paralyzed. You can choose to walk in the strength of the Holy Spirit!

QUESTIONS TO PONDER

1. *Do you consider yourself a spiritual invalid? Why or why not?*

2. *What are you asking God to heal in your life?*

3. *What is your excuse for not growing spiritually?*

4. *How much faith do you put in God's Word?*

5. *Whose strength do you rely on, yours or God's?*

GOD'S WORD TO YOU

But he said to me, "My grace is sufficient for you, for my power is made perfect in weakness."
2 Corinthians 12:9

DAILY PRAYER

Dear Heavenly Father,
No longer will I live like a spiritual invalid! I choose to receive the strength that You have for me, that I may "pick up my mat" and walk in the power and strength of the Holy Spirit that You offer to Your children. Thank You for feeding me Your Word. It's in Jesus name I pray. Amen!

DAY 7

To Whom Much Is Given
By Lisa

Are you being a good steward of what God has given to you? God has given us houses, cars, jobs, clothes, kids, spouses and lots of other things to watch over. He also gives us talents and gifts that He wants us to use as we go through life. So are you being a good steward, or caretaker, of the things God has given to you? Think about your prayer time this past week. What have you been asking God for? Is it something God has already given to you, but you've decided you need another one or a different one, or is it something you really do need? I believe God finds joy in giving to His children, but He also expects us to take care of what He has given to us so that we can continue to handle more and more responsibility for His kingdom as we prove ourselves worthy.

There is a parable in Matthew 24:45-51 where we are told that a faithful servant who does what the master expects him to would be put in charge of all his master's possessions as he follows his master's will. Whereas the wicked servant who didn't do what the master had asked, on the master's unexpected arrival, would be severely punished and put with the hypocrites where there is weeping and gnashing of teeth. We want to be the faithful servant, doing God's will and being put in charge of more and more.

Is there an area of new responsibility that has come to you because you have been faithful to what God has asked you to do, or are you in the middle of a commitment that you'd like to get out of? If you accepted that commitment because that's what God wanted you to do, then stick with it and see it through to the end. If you have a new responsibility from God, then take it on knowing that God will bless you for your commitment.

When you look at all that you have – all that God has given to you, do you realize that to whom much is given, from him much will be required?

> *"...From everyone who has been given much, much will be demanded; and from the one who has been entrusted with much, much more will be asked."*
> —Luke 12:48

What is God requiring of you? What has God already given to you that needs some attention? If you got what you've been praying for, would you have to spend more time on its upkeep than you currently have to give? If you're like me, I'm sure you've thought of a few things that need some extra attention in your life. I am certainly convicted of some things I've let go for far too long. I know I need the Father's help to become the best steward I can be so that I can use what God has given me to serve Him better. In His time, we will be asked to do more for Him and have more responsibility toward His kingdom as we are faithful to take care of the people, the gifts and talents, and all the material things He has given to us.

QUESTIONS TO PONDER

1. *What kind of a steward are you with what God has given you?*

2. *Are you being faithful with what you have committed to?*

3. *Is God requiring much from you because much has been given to you?*

4. *What has God given to you to take care of?*

GOD'S WORD TO YOU

His master replied, "Well done, good and faithful servant! You have been faithful with a few things; I will put you in charge of many things. Come and share your master's happiness!"
Matthew 25:23

DAILY PRAYER

Dear Heavenly Father,
I want to be the good steward that You want me to be. Please give me the strength and determination to stick with those things You've called me to do. And help me to use the gifts and talents that You've given me in a way that would honor and glorify You. Father, I want to be a good and faithful servant to You. Thank You for giving me so much. Help me to appreciate all that You've done for me. In Jesus name I pray. Amen.

DAY 8

What Does Your Future Hold?
By Lisa

What do you do when you need guidance for the future? Do you go to your daily horoscope, or maybe you call the psychic hot-line or look to fortune-tellers? Why do you look to things that are not of God for answers that can only come from God? In Deuteronomy 18:10-13 we find out just how God feels about these things and those who practice them: *" Let no one be found among you who sacrifices his son or daughter in the fire, who practices divination or sorcery, interprets omens, engages in witchcraft, [11]or casts spells, or who is a medium or spiritist or who consults the dead. [12]Anyone who does these things is detestable to the LORD, and because of these detestable practices the LORD your God will drive out those nations before you. [13]You must be blameless before the LORD your God."*

Why do you think God finds these things so detestable? Maybe it's because when you look to them for your future, you are not looking to God. You are removing God from your life when you seek other things to tell you your future, no matter how harmless they may seem. Anything that replaces God is an idol, which is sin.

It's a serious matter for us just as it was a serious matter for King Saul in 1 Samuel 28 when he consulted a medium to find out his future with a war against the Philistines. It was after the time of Samuel's death, and Saul knew that the Spirit of the Lord had left him. Saul tells us that God wasn't answering his inquiries, so Saul decided to take matters into his own hands. He consulted a medium who could bring Samuel up from the dead to give him the guidance he needed. Now Saul knew that it was against God's law to go to a medium. In fact, he had put most of the mediums and spiritists out of the land, but there was still one, the medium at En Dor. This medium brought Samuel up from the dead, and Saul inquired of him what he should do. But what he found out was that he and his sons were going to die the next day. Consulting Samuel through the medium didn't help Saul a bit, it only made him afraid. In the end, *"Saul died because he was unfaithful to the Lord; he did not keep the word of the Lord and even consulted a medium for guidance, and did not inquire of the Lord..."* (1 Chronicles 10:13) It's interesting to see from this Scripture that Saul never really had inquired of the Lord.

Maybe you feel like Saul, that God isn't answering your prayers. My first question would be, do you really know the Lord? Do you have a personal relationship with God through His Son, Jesus Christ? In the old covenant, before Jesus was resurrected, the Spirit of God would come and go from people. But in the new covenant, when you receive Jesus as your Lord and Savior, you are sealed with the Holy Spirit (Eph 4:30). If you already have a personal relationship with Jesus, have you actually asked God for an answer? Or maybe you are knowingly living in sin? God has already forgiven you of all your sins – past, present and future. When you truly understand this, it makes hearing from God much easier. If you're still not hearing from God, then you should wait for Him to answer. Or perhaps what He's saying by not answering you is, "Not right now, I have something better in mind." So many times we want an answer right away, and that's not always God's timing or His will for us. Sometimes He just wants us to wait on Him.

What does your future hold? The only true answer to that is what God wants to reveal to you. Put your trust in God alone. Read His Word to find out all that He has in store for you as you follow His will. You will find you have no need for horoscopes, psychics, fortune-tellers, or anything else *but* God.

QUESTIONS TO PONDER

1. Who or what do you go to for guidance?

2. Do you believe God has a good plan for your life?

3. Do you ask God for His guidance?

4. If God is not answering your prayers, why do you think that is?

5. Are you trusting God for your life?

GOD'S WORD TO YOU

"For I know the plans I have for you," declares the LORD, "plans to prosper you and not to harm you, plans to give you hope and a future."
Jeremiah 29:11

DAILY PRAYER

Dear Heavenly Father,
Open my eyes of understanding, Lord. Walk before me and help me to ask You for direction. I trust You and You alone for my future. Thank You for already forgiving me for looking to anything or anyone other than You and godly counsel for direction for my life. In Jesus name I pray. Amen.

DAY 9

The Temple of God
By Cindy

The book of Ezra begins with the first wave of Jews returning to Jerusalem to rebuild the temple. The first thing they did when they got to Jerusalem was to build an altar on the foundation of the old altar. They built the altar first so that they could reconnect with and return to a relationship with God.

Now that they were able to be obedient to God through the sacrifices, it was time to begin work on rebuilding the temple. Just like anything in life, if you are doing what God wants you to Satan doesn't like it and will try anything to stop you from being obedient. So, as the Jews started rebuilding the temple, the people that lived in the area first acted really nice to them in order to infiltrate their ranks and hinder the workers. When that didn't work, they decided to go straight to the top and sent a letter to the Persian king to remind him that all through history the Jewish people rebelled against their kings and if the temple got rebuilt, they'd continue with their rebellious ways. The king immediately ordered a halt to the rebuilding and not another stone was laid *for fifteen years.*

So, while the idle Jews had nothing to build; they (and even their priests) began to accept the ideology of the people that lived in the area. Slowly they began to forget about the Laws of Moses and even started acting like pagans themselves. Satan, the great deceiver, was dancing in the streets, but he didn't count on Ezra coming along. Ezra was a teacher who was well versed in the Law of Moses and the hand of the Lord was upon him. When Ezra got to Jerusalem, he reminded the Jews of who they were and he showed them how they were sinning against God. Because the people were living under the Old Covenant the only way for them to turn back to God and give their hearts once again to Him was through repentance of their sins.

To the Jews, their stone and mortar temple was where God was. We are told in 1 Corinthians 6:19, *"Do you not know that your body is a temple of the Holy Spirit, who is in you, whom you have received from God? You are not your own."* If you are a Christian, your body is the temple of God. God lives within you and has a direct relationship with you!

How is your temple? Are there any cracks in the mortar? Has the influence of the surrounding community infiltrated and gotten you off the task of building up and strengthening your temple? Take a moment and look around at the outside influences that may be trying to hinder God's work from being completed in your life. What is getting in your way of having a complete relationship with God?

The Jews needed Ezra to show them the error of their ways. You have God living in you! Take the time right now and ask Him to show you the weak spots in your temple walls and when He does, don't hesitate and don't argue, just repair those weak spots with the special mortar of remembering who you are in Christ *and* then seek to stay connected with God by *knowing* that you are righteous because of the completed work of Christ on the cross.

> *"Search me, O God, and know my heart; test me and know my anxious thoughts. ^{24}See if there is any offensive way in me, and lead me in the way everlasting."*
>
> —Psalm 139:23-24.

QUESTIONS TO PONDER

1. *The Jews stopped building on their temple for 15 years. How is the building of your temple coming along?*

2. *The Jews needed the temple to make sacrifices to God. What have you sacrificed to God?*

3. *God has a purpose and a plan for each of us. What has God asked you to build that you've stopped working on?*

4. *Are you steadily working on your temple or are you conforming to the world around you?*

GOD'S WORD TO YOU

The LORD looks down from heaven on the sons of men to see if there are any who understand, any who seek God.
Psalm 14:2

DAILY PRAYER

Dear Father God,
As a Christian, I know that the Holy Spirit resides in me. Lord, forgive me for the many times that I have not recognized that fact. Forgive me, Lord, for the times that I stopped building Your temple in my life. Father, I ask that You forgive me for the times that I have allowed the surrounding community to infiltrate the cracks of my temple and caused me to stop building up and strengthening my temple. Lord, I ask that Your Holy Spirit living within me always keep me focused on Your Son and always keep me growing in Christ. Father, I know that I am the righteousness of God in Christ! In the name of Jesus Christ I pray. Amen!

DAY 10

It Is Well With My Soul
By Cindy

In the Jewish temple there was an innermost sanctuary called the Holy of Holies and this is where the Ark of the Covenant was kept. This is where God resided (Exodus 25:8). When the priest entered the Holy of Holies, he was entering into the very presence of God. Because of the sacrifice that Jesus Christ made for us when He died upon the cross, if you are a Christ follower, you now have the very presence of God living within you through the Holy Spirit. You are a walking Holy of Holies!

When we often hear devotionals and sermons about our bodies as the temple of God (1Corinthians 6:19), it usually refers to how well we keep our bodies through exercise, eating the right kind of foods, staying away from alcohol, drugs, smoking and other abuses of our bodies. What I am writing about today is your soul! Everybody has a soul. You exist because of your soul. Your soul will never die and your soul will spend eternity in one of two places....heaven or hell! Jesus tells us in Matthew 25:46, *"Then they will go away to eternal punishment, but the righteous to eternal life."* Without a personal relationship with Jesus Christ, your soul's eternal destination is hell.

It is so easy to forget that not only is your body a temple of God, but your soul is a direct pipeline to the throne of God! Can you imagine? Because the Holy Spirit resides in you and you have direct access to God Almighty, you are allowed to walk into His throne room, crawl up onto His lap, and ask Him to hold you and to listen to you as you pour your heart out to Him! He is *always accessible to you*, He never turns you away and He is always there for you!

In the *Temple of God* devotional yesterday, as I wrote about rebuilding your temple, I was thinking about your soul....How is your soul? Does it need repair? You feed your body to nourish it. Are you nourishing your soul? Are you allowing your soul to commune daily with God? We get so preoccupied with our busy selves that sometimes we forget that our soul needs to be refreshed. As Christians you and I need that soul refreshing. We need the repair to our souls that only close fellowship with God can give us. Satan knows that when we spend time in God's Word and when we continuously pray and dialogue with God we are thinking about eternal things and not about the here and now, or in other words, worldly things. Satan wants to keep us so busy with unimportant things that we forget to nourish and refresh our souls. I'm not trying to trivialize our busy lives as unimportant, but when compared to eternity....shouldn't the repair of our souls be the only thing that matters to us?

In 1873, Horatio Spafford wrote the words to the song, *"It is Well with My Soul."*[4] Mrs. Spafford and their 4 daughters were on a ship crossing the Atlantic when the ship sank rapidly after colliding with another ship. Mrs. Spafford sent a telegram back to Horatio with only 2 words, "Saved Alone!" Hurrying to be with his grieving wife, he wrote the words when the ship he was on passed very close to the place where all 4 of his daughters died. Can you imagine how Horatio must have felt when he wrote the comforting words of this song? *"And Lord, haste the day when my faith shall be sight, The clouds be rolled back as a scroll; The trump shall resound, and the Lord shall descend, Even so, It is well with my soul."*[5]

This week as you go about your busy schedule, take some time to reflect on the condition of your soul. Does it need rebuilding and restoring? Do you need to boldly walk into God's throne room and crawl upon God's lap? Do you need God to just hold you quietly in His arms for a few minutes? Can you tell me......is it well with your soul?

QUESTIONS TO PONDER

1. In what way can you allow God to refresh your soul? What is the most effective way God uses to nourish your soul?

2. Take a moment and reflect upon your soul's condition. Can you honestly say that all is well with your soul?

3. How often do you spend time refreshing your soul?

4. Do you realize that you are a walking Holy of Holies and that God, through the Holy Spirit, resides in you? Describe in your own words what that means to you.

GOD'S WORD TO YOU

Come to me, all you who are weary and burdened, and I will give you rest. Take my yoke upon you and learn from me, for I am gentle and humble in heart, and you will find rest for your souls.
Matthew 11:28-29

DAILY PRAYER

Dear Father God,
Thank You so much, Lord, for Your Holy Spirit that comforts me, teaches me, grows me, refreshes me and gives rest to my soul. I'm so thankful, Father, that because of Your Holy Spirit, I am never alone and You are always with me. In Your precious Son's name, I pray! Amen.

DAY 11

Me, A Priest?
By Lisa

Have you ever thought about being a part of a holy priesthood? God tells us in His Word that as believers, *we* are a holy priesthood.

> *"...you also, like living stones, are being built into a spiritual house to be a holy priesthood, offering spiritual sacrifices acceptable to God through Jesus Christ."*
>
> —1 Peter 2:5

Now you may think, "How can *I* be a holy priest?" Think about the duties of a priest back in the days of the temple. Their main focus was to minister to the Lord, and as a part of the priesthood, your focus should be to minister to the Lord as well.

> *"And you shall anoint Aaron and his sons, and consecrate them, that they may minister to Me as priests."*
>
> —Exodus 30:30

Priests were also consecrated, or set apart, for God's purposes. Their consecration included the washing of their body, which is symbolic of when a new believer is washed by the blood of Jesus after they have accepted Christ as their Lord and Savior. We are made spiritually clean and are set apart for God's purposes when we accept Christ.

Have you accepted Jesus as your Lord and Savior? Have you been washed clean by the blood of Jesus?

The priests also offered up sacrifices to God. As believers, part of our ministry to God is to offer up spiritual sacrifices to Him. There are all types of sacrifices we can make to God. We can give of our time, our money, and our possessions. We can also make sacrifices to God by being obedient to Him and staying in His Word. The priests made daily sacrifices to the Lord. What sacrifice is He asking you to make? And is there anything stopping you from being obedient? Ask God to remove any obstacles that are keeping you from God's will for your life.

The priests were also commanded to keep the oil in the Golden Lampstand of the temple burning from evening until morning. In the bible, oil represents the Holy Spirit. As believers, we are sealed with the Holy Spirit and have access to His light. Ministering to the Lord daily will keep your inner fire burning bright!

Everything that the priests did while ministering to the Lord was an act of worship. We can live our lives as an act of worship to the Lord each day. How do you currently minister to the Lord and what can you do differently to minister to Him every day? Think about some of the jobs you do throughout the day and offer them up as a sacrifice of praise to God. Don't complain about them, but do them as if you were doing them for God (1 Corinthians 10:31). That could really change the way you do the dishes or the laundry or any job that you're not particularly fond of!

As a believer in Christ, you are a part of His holy priesthood. You are holy because God made you holy.

Now it's time to ask God to get your heart where it needs to be – focused upon the Lord to minister to Him every day!

QUESTIONS TO PONDER

1. How are you ministering to God and to others?

2. What can you do this day as an act of worship to the Lord?

3. What do you think it means "to do everything as if you were doing it for God?" (Colossians 3:23)

4. Describe in your own words what it means to you to minister to God as a priest.

5. What sacrifice is He asking you to make today?

GOD'S WORD TO YOU

Therefore by Him let us continually offer the sacrifice of praise to God, that is, the fruit of our lips, giving thanks to His name.
Hebrews 13:15 (NKJV)

DAILY PRAYER

Dear Heavenly Father,
Thank You for adding me to Your holy priesthood. Lord, show me ways that I can minister to You each day. You are worthy of my devotion and my praise! Strengthen me and help me to be obedient to You no matter what the cost. Remove any obstacles that are keeping me from Your will. Please help me to bring my daily sacrifice to Your altar – a sacrifice that is pleasing to You. Show me what that sacrifice is for today. In Jesus name I pray. Amen.

DAY 12

A Penny for Your Thoughts
By Lisa

Has anyone ever asked you, "A penny for your thoughts?" Maybe you were deep in thought and they were just wondering what was going on in that head of yours. The real question is, have you ever stopped to think about what you are thinking about? Our right thoughts are the beginning to a transformed life!

> *"Do not conform any longer to the patterns of this world, but be transformed by the renewing of your mind."*
> —Romans 12:2

How is your mind renewed? It's renewed when you take your thoughts captive to the obedience of Christ.

> *"For though we walk in the flesh, we do not war according to the flesh. For the weapons of our warfare are not carnal, but mighty in God for pulling down strongholds, casting down arguments and every high thing that sets itself up against the knowledge of God, bringing every thought captive to the obedience of Christ."*
> —2 Corinthians 10:3-5

Do you want to know how to take a thought captive? You think about what you're thinking about! And not only do you think about what you're thinking about, but you do it over and over and over again. As believers in Christ, we don't war in a carnal or fleshly way like the world does, we war spiritually. To take thoughts "captive" you restrain them like you would restrain a prisoner. Interrogate your thought and see where it came from and where it's going. Does it have any business there? Is this thought going to glorify God? Is it going to bring life to you or another person? Or is this thought going to bring discouragement and destruction which can lead to death? We've got to think about what we're thinking about!

The spiritual weapons of God pull down those well-fortified strongholds. We need strongholds when it comes to the truths of God's Word, but it's those places that we believe a lie that need to be torn down. These are the type of strongholds that need to go. The Greek word used for "pulling down" in verse 4 above is literally talking about demolishing a fortress. To demolish these strongholds, the Word of God is like a hammer. It will smash down the lies, which are the high things that set themselves up against the knowledge of God. If something is spoken against God's knowledge, then obviously, it's a lie because God is not able to lie (Hebrews 6:18).

When we finish interrogating the thoughts we've been thinking, we have two choices. We can either accept the thought or reject it. By accepting the good thoughts and rejecting the thoughts that go against God, we are bringing every thought captive "to the obedience of Christ". If the thought isn't obedient to Christ then it goes. If it is obedient, then it should stay. The trouble we get into is when we let thoughts stay that should go. These thoughts cause issues like unforgiveness, bitterness, envy, pride, jealousy, hatred, anger, etc. and cause us to be a captive to the enemy, which is disobedience to Christ.

Have you been thinking about what you're thinking about? What are you doing with those thoughts that are coming into your mind? Are they pleasing to God? Are they creating life? If your interrogation shows they're not, then cast them down! We have the mind of Christ (1 Corinthians 2:16), let's use it in a way that honors Him!

QUESTIONS TO PONDER

1. *How often do you think about what you're thinking about?*

2. *What kind of thoughts are you thinking about?*

3. *Would God be pleased with the thoughts you dwell on?*

4. *How often do you use the "hammer" of God's Word to tear down strongholds in your life?*

5. *How do you cast down your thoughts?*

GOD'S WORD TO YOU

*For who has known the mind of the Lord
that he may instruct him?
But we have the mind of Christ.*
1 Corinthians 2:16

DAILY PRAYER

Dear Heavenly Father,
Thank You for giving me the wisdom and understanding from Your Word to help me determine which thoughts should stay and which should go. Thank You for the Holy Spirit who guides me. And thank You for tearing down the lies that I have been believing with the hammer of Your Word. I choose to think on those things that are pleasing to You. In Jesus name I pray. Amen.

DAY 13

How Is Your Foundation?
By Cindy

During the summer in the state of Texas, it's not uncommon to hear that people are having foundation issues with their houses. Due to the excessive heat that we have here, the clay soil contracts and moves from around and under buildings which in turn removes the support that the building needs and then part of the building will often settle to the lower elevation. This settling then causes cracks to appear in the walls. I saw a commercial for a foundation repair company the other day and it got me to thinking about my foundation. I wasn't thinking about the foundation of my house, but I was thinking about the foundation that was laid many years ago concerning my faith.

In Matthew 7:24-27, Jesus tells us a parable of two builders, a wise man and a foolish man. *"Therefore everyone who hears these words of mine and puts them into practice is like a wise man who built his house on the rock. [25]The rain came down, the streams rose, and the winds blew and beat against that house; yet it did not fall, because it had its foundation on the rock. [26]But everyone who hears these words of mine and does not put them into practice is like a foolish man who built his house on sand. [27]The rain came down, the streams rose, and the winds blew and beat against that house, and it fell with a great crash."*

I love this parable. To me it really paints a picture. I can easily see the rain and hear the wind beating against the house; I can see the streams rising and the house crashing down. But, Jesus was not instructing us on where and how to build a house.....He was telling us that our foundation must be built upon Him! Jesus is the solid rock and the material we use to build with is His Word, the Bible. If our foundation is not solid and has any cracks in it, when Satan comes storming against us, the ground will move from under us and our house will come crashing down.

This started me thinking about the foundation that had been laid "unknowingly" for me by my parents (especially my mother) and my church. I look back now on the time that my husband and I lived in Florida and we were out of church, living in the world for 18 years. During that time, in our marriage, we saw heavy rains and we heard the winds slamming against the walls of our house. We felt the house shake, but because of the solid foundation laid years earlier by our individual acceptance of Jesus Christ as our Savior, and because of the biblical teaching we received from our parents and the church.....our house stood and is standing even stronger today.

Sometimes, I wake up singing....Do you ever do that? I woke up the other morning singing:

"His oath, His covenant, His blood
Support me in the whelming flood;
When all around my soul gives way,
He then is all my hope and stay.

On Christ, the solid Rock, I stand;
all other ground is sinking sand,
All other ground is sinking sand."[6]

Christ is the solid rock! What is your foundation built on....the solid rock or sinking sand?

QUESTIONS TO PONDER

1. Read Matthew 7:24-27 again. Are you like the wise man or the foolish man?

2. What is your foundation built on - solid rock or sinking sand?

3. Do you feel like your house is crashing down because of bad choices you've made? What can you do differently to change your foundation to be built upon the rock?

4. Describe in your own words what it means to have a strong spiritual foundation?

GOD'S WORD TO YOU

He said: "The LORD is my rock, my fortress and my deliverer; my God is my rock, in whom I take refuge, my shield and the horn of my salvation. He is my stronghold, my refuge and my savior–from violent men you save me.
2 Sam 22:2-3

DAILY PRAYER

Dear Father God,
I thank You so much, Lord, for those in my past who loved me enough to lay a solid foundation for me even when I couldn't possibly understand the eternal implications. Father, I pray that You use me in the lives of the people that I touch that I would lay a foundation for them that would be grounded in Christ. I thank You, Father, that You loved me enough to send Your Son, Jesus, to die on the cross for me because He is my only hope. He is the solid rock of my soul's foundation. I ask this in Jesus' name! Amen

DAY 14

Jack-in-the-Box God
By Lisa

Do you remember the little musical Jack-in-the-box toys? You'd wind the box while the music played and then suddenly a clown would pop out of the box, scaring you half to death! Then you'd push him back into the box and close the lid so you could do it all over again!

This is how I picture the way we Christians treat God. We limit God by putting Him in a box. We treat Him like He's a Jack-in-the-box! We stuff God into this nice little box that we've decided He should fit in, and then we go along our merry way to the tune in our own head. Then every now and then He shows Himself to be a big God and pops out of the box, scaring us half to death! So we cram Him back in the box and close the lid to start all over again.

God is a big God no matter how hard we try to make Him fit into our own preconceived ideas. God tells us in Isaiah 55:8-9, *"For my thoughts are not your thoughts, neither are your ways my ways... As the heavens are higher than the earth, so are my ways higher than your ways and my thoughts than your thoughts."*

I'd rather have a big God who scares me a bit and that I don't fully understand, than a small God any day. I want a big, big God! I want a God who knows me better than I know myself. I want a God who is in control of the universe. I want a God who is in control of my life! I want a God who isn't always just a good friend, but who is kind of scary because He is so much bigger that I could ever imagine!

We need to have a healthy fear of God. It seems like, as Christians, we see God as our best buddy, but we have no fear of Him. Having God as a friend is great and it's biblical, but we are missing something when we don't have an appropriate fear of God. This kind of fear of God causes us to be in awe of who He is and what He can do. It reminds me of the great lion, Aslan, who is a symbol of Christ in the book, *"The Chronicles of Narnia"*[7] by C.S. Lewis. When the character, Mr. Beaver is asked if Aslan is safe, he replies, *"Safe? ...Who said anything about safe? 'Course he isn't safe. But he's good. He's the King, I tell you."*

Our King of Kings is good, but is He safe? 'Course He isn't safe! But don't we try to feel safe by limiting Him? You see, we've got it backwards. We fear men and what they will think instead of fearing God. Shouldn't we take heed of Matthew 10:28, where Jesus said, *"Do not be afraid of those who kill the body but cannot kill the soul. Rather, be afraid of the One who can destroy both soul and body in hell."* What Jesus is saying here is don't put your fear in the wrong place. Don't fear man, but instead, have a healthy fear, respect and awe of God.

So let's take God out of the box we've put Him in because He's *way* too big for that! Let's allow Him to be big in our lives, even if it scares us! Besides, we *need* that reverential fear of God! Let's allow Him to grow and stretch us so that we can come to know Him better. God – Be BIG in our lives!

QUESTIONS TO PONDER

1. How are you limiting God by putting Him in a box?

2. In what way is God trying to show you how big He is?

3. How do you show God reverential fear, awe and respect?

4. Why do you think Christians fear men and what they think instead of fearing God? How have you seen this?

5. How could you let God grow and stretch you so that you can come to know Him better?

GOD'S WORD TO YOU

"To whom will you compare me? Or who is my equal?" says the Holy One.
Isaiah 40:25

DAILY PRAYER

Heavenly Father,
Thank You for being a big God. I ask that You move in a big way in my life. Don't let me limit You by putting You in a box. I want to see You moving in ways that are so big, that it couldn't be anybody but You! Thank You for what You have done already, and I look forward to what you are going to do in my future. In Jesus name I pray. Amen!

DAY 15

Lift Up Your Face
By Cindy

I was listening to the song, *"Lift up Your Face"*[8] by Third Day the other day and it got me to thinking about how often I lift up my face to the God of Heaven. How often do any of us actually lift up our face and truly look up into the heavens, peering intently into the sky and actively searching for God?

I've been participating in a Bible Study about David and the study has been about how David was called out and appointed by God to be King of all Israel. I love reading about David's ascension as King and thinking about how even though David made many, many mistakes, he still carried the label as "a man after God's own heart." Acts 13:22 (KJV) says, *"And when he had removed him, he raised up unto them David to be their king; to whom also he gave testimony, and said, I have found David the son of Jesse, a man after mine own heart, which shall fulfill all my will."* I was thinking how awesome it would be to be loved by God that much!

James 4:8 says to us, *"Come near to God and he will come near to you. Wash your hands, you sinners, and purify your hearts, you double-minded."* I'm thinking that God didn't love David any more than he loves you or me because Hebrews chapter 13 verse 8 says,

"Jesus Christ is the same yesterday and today and forever." So now, I'm wondering if the connection here is simply that David loved God more than we do. What do you think?

I think that we have not fully realized that the God we serve today is the same powerful and faithful God of the Old Testament. Sure, if you have been saved by grace then you have a home waiting for you in heaven.....but do you really realize what it means to follow Christ? It means that you have God the Holy Spirit *living within you*! It means that you have the power to resist the devil and he will flee from you (James 4:7)! It means that you have God the Father watching over you! It means that you have Jesus Christ the Living Son of God making plans just for you and willing to direct your every footstep!

All we have to do is be obedient! How hard can that be? It's not that hard if you put God first in your life. It's a choice! It's your choice whether or not you choose to let go and let God have control or whether you choose to continue to do things your way. So, have you really, I mean *really* tried to put Christ first in your life? When I pray, I do pray for my husband and family and friends and hurts and pains, and just like you, I pray for the usual things. But, lately, I find that all I really want to do is thank God for just being my God, for being *who* He is. Mostly, I feel the need to just praise God, instead of asking Him for things. As a parent, do you ever get tired of your children always asking for things? Maybe God feels the same way about us. Matthew 6:8 tells us that God knows all of our needs before we even ask. So instead of asking all of the time, maybe we should just get down on our knees, lift up our faces and just praise God for who He is and thank Him for the blessings that He has given us. Maybe we should voice to God that we really do trust Him and that no matter where life takes us, we will always know that He is in control and that He is always faithful.

I don't want to step on toes here, or sound preachy, but I really want you to see that truly giving your heart over to God is a choice. You have the choice to get up thirty minutes earlier in the morning to spend time in prayer, you have a choice to turn the television off at night to read scripture, and you have the choice to give up things in your life that you know are not of God. That's the great thing about our God! He will take two steps toward us even if we just take one step toward Him. Our God is always faithful and He will always choose to make time for us, even if we choose not to make time for Him.

QUESTIONS TO PONDER

1. When is the last time you actively searched for God?

2. How often do you actually lift up your face and just thank God for who He is and for all that He has done for you?

3. If how much we love God is indicated by how often we draw near to Him, on a scale from 1 to 10, how much do you show you love Him?

4. How often do you thank God and praise Him without asking for anything in return?

GOD'S WORD TO YOU

*I will extol the LORD at all times; his praise
will always be on my lips.*
Psalms 34:1

DAILY PRAYER

*Dear Father God,
Thank You so much, Lord, for being my God! Lord, You are amazing and I am so thankful for all that You have given me, from my very life, down to each and every blessing. Lord, You are Holy and I am so thankful that You have given me life through Your precious Son, Jesus Christ. Guide me, direct me, and help me, Lord, to stay obedient and focused on You. I ask this, Father, in Your precious Son's name! Amen*

DAY 16

"Just" Pray
By Lisa

"...The prayer of a righteous man is powerful and effective."
—James 5:16

How many times have I said, "All I can do is *just* pray for them."? Wow, am I showing what little faith I have in prayer, that all I can do is *just* pray? Haven't I realized the power of prayer? I know I've seen God work through so many of my prayers. How can I not see that the most important and the most powerful thing I can do *is* to pray?

How often do we forget to pray until "all else fails"? What has to happen for us to finally remember to pray first and then do whatever else God calls us to do? We need to take a moment and remember what God has already done in our lives in answer to prayer. When we remember what He's already done, it makes it easier to remember to stop and pray *first* so that we can see what He's *going* to do this time.

We can also stop and pray right away whenever someone asks for our prayers. Instead of saying, "I'll pray for you….", and then walking away–what if you stopped right where you are and prayed for them? Think how it would make them feel if you stopped to pray for them right then and there. Think how encouraging it would be for that person to actually hear your request to God on their behalf. *Imagine* what it would do to their faith when they see God *answer* your prayer!

There is an important point to this verse in James—*"The prayer of a righteous man is powerful and effective"*! So, what makes a person righteous, or in right standing with God? You are made right with God when you accept His Son, Jesus Christ, as your Lord and Savior. (Romans 3:22) When you understand the righteousness that you have as a believer in Christ, then you know that God hears you when you pray. It doesn't matter if your prayers are simple or not. God loves to hear His children pray. Don't feel inadequate just because you are a new believer or because you aren't used to praying in front of people. Remember, Jesus wasn't happy with those who prayed in order to be heard for their many words (Matthew 6:7). And if you have sinned, remember that God has already forgiven you for all your sins, so turn to Him, receive your forgiveness, and move on. You won't have powerful prayers if you're wallowing in self-pity. But you *can* have powerful and effective prayers *because* of your right standing with Christ. Don't "just" pray because all else has failed. Instead, pray *first* because you know your prayers are powerful and effective!

QUESTIONS TO PONDER

1. *How does one have right standing with God?*

2. *What can you do to make prayer more important?*

3. *How can you become a more effective pray-er?*

4. *What can help you to see how powerful your prayers already are?*

5. *What is keeping you from having a powerful prayer life?*

GOD'S WORD TO YOU

For the eyes of the Lord are on the righteous and his ears are attentive to their prayer, but the face of the Lord is against those who do evil.
1 Peter 3:12

DAILY PRAYER

Dear Heavenly Father,
Thank You for giving me righteousness through belief in Your Son, Jesus, so that my prayers are effective and powerful. Keep me humble knowing that You are the source of all power, and You are the one who provides for all of my needs. In Jesus name I pray. Amen.

DAY 17

Who's Your Enemy?
By Lisa

Think of the person who is causing all sorts of grief and heartache in your life. When you look at all the strife they have caused you and your family, it makes you want to hurt them or hold bitterness or unforgiveness against them deep inside. But when you see who the *real* enemy is, you don't have to try and get back at them or hold unforgiveness or bitterness in your heart.

God tells us who our real enemy is…

> *"For our struggle is not against flesh and blood, but against the rulers, against the authorities, against the powers of this dark world and against the spiritual forces of evil in the heavenly realms."*
> —Ephesians 6:12

The Bible tells us that the "flesh and blood" person who has been hurting us really isn't our enemy. Our enemy is Satan and his demons who tempt people to use their own fleshly desires to wreak havoc in other people's lives. Satan is happy to use people to cause misery and strife in your life and others. And the thing is, if we're not careful, Satan will use us too. None of us like to be used, but part of the problem is that we don't even realize what's happening! *The truth is, we can be used by the enemy just as easily as that other person who's been causing us trouble.* We get this thought that comes to our mind to do something we know isn't right, and instead of pushing that thought away, we entertain it. The next thing you know, we've decided to act on the thought, and when we do, we've just gone from temptation to sin.

To keep from being used by the enemy, you've got to know who your real enemy is. When you know that, then you will understand who's putting those evil thoughts into your mind. And when you realize where those evil thoughts are coming from, you can choose not to act on them.

We don't want to be used by Satan, but there is One that we do want to be used by, and that's God! Our hearts desire is to be used by God. He is the only one who will not hurt us by using us because when we are used by God it is for our good and the good of others.

When you think of the reason people do what they do to hurt us, it makes it a whole lot easier to do what Jesus asks us to do in Matthew 5:44 and 46. Jesus said, *"...Love your enemies and pray for those who persecute you... If you love those who love you, what reward will you get?"*

Jesus wants us to love our enemies and pray for them. The best way to get back at the tempter, Satan, is to love others and pray for them, even when they've hurt us. You'll find that when you pray for your enemy, the unforgiveness and bitterness you have toward them will subside until it eventually goes away. Only Jesus is able to take away the pain and give us a love for those who've hurt us. Remember, we were once an enemy of God before accepting Jesus as our Lord and Savior, and Jesus prayed for us and intercedes on our behalf. (John 17:20-26, Hebrews 7:25) How can we do any less for our enemies?

QUESTIONS TO PONDER

1. *Who have you been looking at as an enemy?*

2. *When you realize that Satan is the real enemy, how does this make you change your thinking about others?*

3. *When was the last time you were used by the enemy to upset someone else? What can you do to stop from being used in that way?*

4. *Who do you need to show love to and pray for?*

5. *Who have you been holding bitterness and unforgiveness toward? Start the process now of forgiveness toward that person and allow Jesus to free you from the bitterness that's been holding you captive.*

GOD'S WORD TO YOU

Bear with each other and forgive whatever grievances you may have against one another. Forgive as the Lord forgave you.
Colossians 3:13

DAILY PRAYER

Dear Heavenly Father,
I thank You for showing me who my enemy really is. Help me to forgive others like You forgave me. Show me where I have offended others so that I can make things right. Give me a love for others that have hurt me. And thank You for forgiving me and interceding on my behalf. In Jesus name. Amen.

DAY 18

Expecting God
By Lisa

So I came out to meet you; I looked for you and have found you!
—Proverbs 7:15

What would life be like if we *truly expected* encounters with God? What if we expected to hear from God every morning when we got up to pray and read in His Word? What if we expected to hear God speak to us in every sermon we listened to? What if we looked for God in the creation around us and expected to see Him there? What if we looked for God in our good and our bad circumstances and expected to see His hand in our lives? What if we expected God to work miracles?

Why don't we expect more encounters with God? Is it because we keep God in a box? I wonder if He allows us to limit Him depending on our belief?

Let's ask God to remove the scales from our eyes (Acts 9:18) that have kept us blinded to His work in our lives. Let's be thankful to God for the many blessings He has given to us. Let's not look only to what God can give *to* us, but what God can do *through* us.

You know, sometimes I can be a real pessimist. For example, let's say I don't want my kids to be disappointed about whether something will happen or not, so instead of hoping (and expecting) for the best case scenario, I set expectations for the worst case scenario so they won't be disappointed if it doesn't happen the way we expect. Then, if things work out better than the worst case scenario, that's great, and we're not disappointed. And if things work out in the way of the worst case scenario, then we're not so disappointed either. Could it be by doing this I'm training my kids *not* to expect the best, which includes not expecting the best from God? And could it be that I'm training them *not* to hope because it's too disappointing when you hope for something and it doesn't happen? And could it be that by setting my expectations low when it comes to God, that I am hoping *not* to be disappointed just in case God doesn't show up and meet my expectations? Maybe our God is only as big as we allow Him to be and expect Him to be. *If I expect nothing, I can surely achieve it. If I expect great things, only God can achieve it.* Isn't it better to expect great things and achieve less than I expected, than to expect nothing and achieve it?

I want to challenge you as I am challenging myself. Let's ask God to change us to expect to see Him and hear Him more and more in all areas of our life. Let's not hope for the least so we won't be disappointed, let's hope for great things and be on fire when we see God work in amazing ways in our lives! God is moving! Let's expect Him to do more than we have ever expected before!

QUESTIONS TO PONDER

1. How are you limiting God through your unbelief?

2. How are you expecting God to show up in your life?

3. What do you need to change to be more expectant?

4. What great things are you expecting God to do in your life, or are you expecting nothing from God and achieving it?

GOD'S WORD TO YOU

But as for me, I watch in hope for the LORD,
I wait for God my Savior;
my God will hear me.
Micah 7:7

DAILY PRAYER

Dear Heavenly Father,
I want to expect great things from You in all areas of my life. Show me where I am expecting little and so am receiving little. Remove the scales from my eyes that keep me from seeing Your work in my life. I am expecting to see great things from You, Lord. Thank You for working in me and through me. In Jesus name I pray. Amen.

DAY 19

Give Careful Thought
By Cindy

In the Old Testament book of Haggai, the first wave of 50,000 Jewish people had returned to Jerusalem from Babylon in order to rebuild the temple and the city. This small remnant of people eagerly laid the foundation of the temple, but that was as far as they got. The native people surrounding Jerusalem did not want the temple built, and because of "politics" the rebuilding campaign came to a grinding halt. While the authorities worked through the "red tape" the Jewish people decided that maybe this was God's way of telling them that it wasn't time to rebuild....just yet. Maybe God was telling them that they really needed to see to their own needs first...before seeing to His house. Besides, they were so eager to get started on God's temple that they forgot all about their needs, and after all, they did have to live didn't they?

An important question to ask yourself is this... since *when* has God ever said, "See to your own needs first and then, if it is convenient, do what I've commanded you to do?" While the Jewish builders were waiting for the Lord to give them the go ahead, they started building themselves really nice houses to live in. I'm talking luxurious cedar paneled houses! In those days houses made from cedar panel were only connected with royal dwellings. After fourteen years, the people still had not figured it out, so God sent Haggai to deliver this message:

> "Now this is what the LORD Almighty says: "Give careful thought to your ways. [6]You have planted much, but have harvested little. You eat, but never have enough. You drink, but never have your fill. You put on clothes, but are not warm. You earn wages, only to put them in a purse with holes in it. [9]"You expected much, but see, it turned out to be little. What you brought home, I blew away. Why?" declares the LORD Almighty. "Because of my house, which remains a ruin, while each of you is busy with his own house."
> —Haggai 1:5-6, 9.

How often are we guilty of the same thing? How often do we go about our daily lives, chasing after our own ideas, of knowing what is best for us and never asking God even once, "What is it that you want me to do, Lord?" When I was praying about this week's devotional and flipping through my Bible looking for something to write about, God directed me to the above passages because, I believe it is a message for me to learn a very important lesson! God wants to be active in every decision…every detail…every aspect of my life and He wants to be first! I realize now how important it is to get up each morning and ask God, "What do you want me to do today?"

I have my "to-do" list and I know what needs to be done every day…but, I have never asked God, "What do *You* want me to do today?" Is this the same daily question that you need to be asking God? I realize when you work you have to be at your job. God knows that too. In that case, He just might say, *"Turn off the television when you come home tonight and just sit and talk to me."* Who knows what God will say, but if you don't ask Him, you'll never know.

God says, "Give careful thought to your ways!" Until you and I truly put Him first in our lives, we will never receive the full blessings that He wants to give to each of us. We will always plant much, but will harvest little. We will always eat, but never have enough. We will always drink, but never have our fill. We will always put on clothes, but we will never truly be warm and we will always earn wages only to put them in a purse with holes in it.

QUESTIONS TO PONDER

1. When is the last time you asked, "Lord, what do You want me to do today?"

2. How have you given careful thought to your ways? Or what do you need to change to start giving careful thought to your ways?

3. Do you find that you're putting your wages in a purse with holes in it? What does God want you to do differently?

4. Do you allow God to be active in all of your decisions, in every aspect of your life?

GOD'S WORD TO YOU

"For the pagans run after all these things, and your heavenly Father knows that you need them. But seek first his kingdom and his righteousness, and all these things will be given to you as well. Therefore do not worry about tomorrow, for tomorrow will worry about itself. Each day has enough trouble of its own."
Matthew 6:32-34

Trust in the LORD with all your heart and lean not on your own understanding; in all your ways acknowledge him, and he will make your paths straight.
Proverbs 3:5-6

DAILY PRAYER

Dear Father God,
Lord, I want to give careful thought to my ways. I don't want to only be satisfied with just enough to get by. I want You in my everyday life and in every decision that I make. Lord, I know that when You are guiding me, when You are active in my life, and when I am being obedient to Your direction for my life, that I will always have more than enough! I will never have to work only to see my earnings put in a purse with holes in it. In Christ's name I pray. Amen!

DAY 20

Hearing God
By Lisa

I've been taking to heart considering what God wants me to do each day rather than running off and doing what is right in my own mind, and I've found that I've been challenged quite a bit. It's easy to ask God, "What do You want me to do today?" but I find it difficult to stop and listen and wait for His answer.

Listening seems to be a lost art. It takes a conscious effort to focus on someone else. One thing I love about my husband is that when he's watching television and I need to talk to him, he will mute or pause the television so he can hear what I have to say. What that one small act shows me is that he's giving me his undivided attention, and what I have to say is important to him.

So my question is, do we give God the same courtesy? Do we put everything "on hold" so we can hear what God has to say to us because it's important to us? Ah, if only we could "mute" those around us! Well, we know that's not going to happen, so we are going to have to be a little drastic in our measures for hearing God. You may have to get up 30 minutes before everyone else in order to have some quiet time in your home. Or maybe it's a matter of *where* you spend your quiet time with God. You may have to retreat to the bathroom or an actual closet in order to have some privacy and time alone with God. Be *drastic* in what you do to make a quiet time and place for God. Surely, He will see your attempts and bless you for it. For me, the greatest blessing is knowing that the big God of the whole universe is speaking to little ol' me.

Now, here is another question for you to consider.... Do you *really* want to hear from God? Think about that for a minute. If you *really* hear from God, then most likely, He's going to give you something to do. Of course, God may display His love for you, or He may give you comfort, or reveal Himself to you in some other way, but generally, when God speaks, He's got something for you to do. There is an *obedience* factor to hearing God. When you hear God, are you going to take action on what He's given you to do? Are you going to read the Word that He's pointed you to? Are you going to help the person He's asked you to? Are you going to give what He's asked you to give? Are you going to serve where He's asked you to serve? With "hearing" comes *responsibility*. God expects us to act on what He tells us. Jesus tells us in Luke 11:28, *"Blessed rather are those who hear the word of God and obey it."*

There are plenty of people who think they can hear without really hearing. Sometimes I can be one of them! It's like when you're talking to someone and you know they're speaking to you, but the next thing you know you've missed the whole crux of the conversation. You don't have to have your ears plugged to tune others out. We can stare right into someone's face and be a million miles away. Similarly, just turning your face to God isn't always enough. He wants all of your attention and He wants you to turn your heart to Him and listen with your heart. Take time to focus on Him. Be still before Him… *Be still and know that He is God.* (Psalm 46:10) Listen… I think He's speaking to you… What is He saying to your heart? And what are you going to do about it?

QUESTIONS TO PONDER

1. Do your actions show that you believe you can hear from God?

2. Do you find it difficult to stop, wait, and listen for God? What can you change to make this better?

3. How are you showing God that you want to hear from Him and that's it's important to you?

4. Where can you go to find a quiet place to be alone with God?

5. What is the last thing God spoke to you, and have you obeyed Him? If not, why not?

GOD'S WORD TO YOU

*In the morning, O LORD, you hear my voice;
in the morning I lay my requests before you
and wait in expectation.*
Psalm 5:3

DAILY PRAYER

*Dear Heavenly Father,
I want, so much, to hear You, Lord. Show me how to hear You more clearly. Show me how to get rid of the distractions so I can have more intimate times with You. My heart is inclined toward You. I wait in expectation to see what You have to say to me this day. In Jesus name I pray. Amen.*

DAY 21

Through the Pain
By Lisa

> "Then I saw a new heaven and a new earth, for the first heaven and the first earth had passed away, and there was no longer any sea. ^{2}I saw the Holy City, the new Jerusalem, coming down out of heaven from God, prepared as a bride beautifully dressed for her husband. ^{3}And I heard a loud voice from the throne saying, 'Now the dwelling of God is with men, and he will live with them. They will be his people, and God himself will be with them and be their God. ^{4}He will wipe every tear from their eyes. There will be no more death or mourning or crying or pain, for the old order of things has passed away.'"
>
> —Revelation 21:1-4

Can you just imagine the time when there will be no more pain – no more crying or mourning or death? That really made me start thinking… What would life be like here on earth without pain? As much as pain hurts, without it, in this day and age, we would probably self-destruct. Pain tells us when something is wrong. It tells us to draw back from the heat. It tells us our bodies need rest. Sometimes we think it's better not to feel the pain than to go through it, so some turn to drugs or alcohol to numb the pain. But in order to heal you have to go *through* the pain. Pain can be our teacher, if we'll let it, and that's actually a good thing.

I was the type of kid who preferred to learn from other's mistakes. I'd much rather watch what my brother and sister did and then make sure I didn't do anything they did that had negative consequences. When I saw someone get burned, I figured, "Why should I have to get burned myself?" I would much rather learn from what other people suffer.

Most of us are pretty good about listening to pain, especially pain in our body. Why is it, then, that it seems we listen to the warnings of pain more than we listen to God's warnings? When God tells us not to do something, His warnings tell us that to continue on will bring pain. It's not that God doesn't want us to do anything fun, it's that He's protecting us. He only warns us not to do those things that will hurt us. He doesn't want us to go through pain any more than we would want our own child to go through pain. As parents, *we* would rather be the one in pain than to see our child in pain. And that's exactly what Jesus did for us. He took our sins…our pain, upon Himself on the cross so that we wouldn't have to suffer. But some of us have to learn the hard way.

In the end, the ultimate pain will be separation from God. Do you really want to experience that pain yourself? You don't have to. The only real way to heal your pain is through Jesus. You don't have to go through the pain alone. And one day, whether in this life or in eternity, you will find that, with Jesus, you have made it *through the pain.*

QUESTIONS TO PONDER

1. *What is causing you pain right now? Imagine a time when that pain is gone. How would it feel to be without pain?*

2. *When was the last time you were in pain, and what did you learn from that pain?*

3. *What are you relying on to get through the pain? If your answer was not God, what can you do to start going to God to help you get through your pain instead of substituting any number of things to help relieve the pain?*

4. *Can you see how you've grown through your pain as you rely on God?*

5. *As a Christian, when you are in the middle of a painful situation, do you call upon the Holy Spirit to give you strength, or do you try to go it alone?*

GOD'S WORD TO YOU

Resist him, standing firm in the faith, because you know that your brothers throughout the world are undergoing the same kind of sufferings. And the God of all grace, who called you to his eternal glory in Christ, after you have suffered a little while, will himself restore you and make you strong, firm and steadfast.
1 Peter 5:9-10

DAILY PRAYER

Dear Heavenly Father,
You know my pain, hurts and troubles. I am thankful that I can rely on You to help me through them. Thank You for being a God who cares about me, and for helping me to grow spiritually. I look forward to the day when there will be no more pain or death or tears, but in the meantime, I have You to help me through. In Jesus name I pray. Amen.

DAY 22

You Can't Fool God!
By Cindy

The other day I passed by this little church and on the marquee was written, *"You Can Fool Yourself, But You Can't Fool God."* Well, that got me to thinking how we think that we are in our own little world and nobody knows what we are doing but us. Then often times we try to fool ourselves by thinking, "Well, just this once won't hurt me."

Many, many times, I have started a diet and each time, I've said, "OK God, this time I'm going to do it!" Well, wasn't that a contract that I was making with God? He knew what I said to Him and then He watched me as (probably not even a day later) I said, "I've got to have this candy bar. Who's going to know it? Besides, I promise I will really get back on my diet tomorrow." When I said, "Who's going to know it?" God did!

Has there ever been a time at your work when you accidentally brought home a pen and said, "Oh, I'll take it back tomorrow", or, "Oh well, they'll never miss it." But, God saw, God knew. Or what about things you "accidentally" view on the internet or what you watch on television? Your spouse or children may not know, but God does. We're all familiar with the quote attributed to Abraham Lincoln: *"You can fool some of the people all of the time, and all of the people some of the time, but you cannot fool all of the people all of the time."*[9] Well, I'm here to tell you that you can NEVER fool God! If you are a Christian, you have God living within you. You have the Holy Spirit literally taking up residence inside you....wherever you go, whatever you see. Whatever you think or do.....you drag the Holy Spirit along with you.

I've been thinking about the Holy Spirit a lot lately and wondering exactly what it means to grieve the Holy Spirit. God wants us to follow His commands and be obedient to Him, but when we ignore Him and constantly sin against Him, I believe that grieves the Holy Spirit within us. As I said, He goes with us everywhere, sees everything we do and hears every thought we have.

Truthfully, when I broke my diet by having the piece of candy, who was I really fooling? Was I fooling myself?...No. I knew exactly what I was doing. Was I fooling God?...No. He knew exactly what I was doing. By stating that I would really get back on my diet tomorrow, I fooled neither one of us.

If you are a Christian, you are not living in your own little world, you have God living within you. If you are not a Christian you're still not living in your own little world because you have God watching everything that you do....He's not living in you, but He is watching your every move. So you're still not fooling anyone.

> "Where can I go from your Spirit? Where can I flee from your presence? ^{8}If I go up to the heavens, you are there; if I make my bed in the depths, you are there. ^{9}If I rise on the wings of the dawn, if I settle on the far side of the sea, ^{10}even there your hand will guide me, your right hand will hold me fast. ^{11}If I say, "Surely the darkness will hide me and the light become night around me, ^{12}even the darkness will not be dark to you; the night will shine like the day, for darkness is as light to you."
> —Psalm 139:7-12

So tell me, *who*, exactly are you fooling?

QUESTIONS TO PONDER

1. *How are you trying to fool yourself? God?*

2. *Is God living in you or is He only watching over you? Do you know the difference?*

3. *Think of a time in your life when you did something that you thought no one knew about. How does it make you feel to know that God knew?*

4. *How does it make you feel to know that you can NEVER fool God? Do you ever think that He is consciously aware of your every move?*

5. *If you are a Christian you have the Holy Spirit living within you. How do you feel when you realize that everywhere you go, He goes, every thought you think, He knows, and everything you see, He sees?*

GOD'S WORD TO YOU

"O LORD, you have searched me and you know me. You know when I sit and when I rise; you perceive my thoughts from afar. You discern my going out and my lying down; you are familiar with all my ways. Before a word is on my tongue you know it completely, O LORD. You hem me in–behind and before; you have laid your hand upon me."
Psalm 139:1-5

DAILY PRAYER

Dear Father God,
I am so tired of running, dear Lord! I am so tired of trying to fool everyone including myself and You, Father. Help me, Lord, to live my life in the open and not in the shadows. Dear Lord, please grant me the strength to live my life for You and to be obedient to the plans that You have called me to. Lord, please forgive me if I have been living a life that grieves Your Holy Spirit. Guide me and direct me to become the child that You have always planned for me to be! In your precious Son Jesus Christ's name, I pray! Amen!

DAY 23

Soaking Up the Word
By Lisa

One day, I had a little mishap with my bible. Somehow I put a bottle of water that wasn't completely closed into the bag that holds my bible. When I found my bible later that day, the water bottle was empty and the top half of my bible was soaked. I was saddened by this, but in my spirit I knew that God would use this situation for my good. (Romans 8:28 – *And we know that in all things God works for the good of those who love Him, who have been called according to His purpose.*) I started ironing out the pages one by one to see if it would help. I felt compelled to continue ironing, as though God had something for me to see in those soggy, crinkled pages. But by the time I got to the book of Joshua, I noticed that the "ironed" pages were sticking out just as much or more than the pages I hadn't yet touched! This entire situation made me think how special the words of the bible really are. They are as relevant today as they were when they were originally written. Through its pages I can relate the stories and characters to me and my life. It's so amazing how God uses His Word to speak to us.

I've read the bible before when it was just a book of words, dry and stale. I've also read the bible when it came to life and flooded my heart. I was like a sponge that couldn't get saturated with enough water. I couldn't get enough of God's Word! It came alive to me because God spoke to me through it. The words in it renewed my mind and changed me. The Word of God truly is living and active and sharper than a double-edged sword, it penetrates even to dividing soul and spirit, joints and marrow; it judges the thoughts and attitudes of the heart. (Hebrews 4:12)

If you find when you read the Word that it seems old and stale to you, make sure you truly know the One who wrote the book. I question whether I truly knew Him at all when His Word was stale to me. I certainly didn't have a personal relationship with Him at that time. When I came to know Him personally, then His Word opened up to me. At that point, I did some of these things, which might help you too…

- First, pray to God that He would make His Word alive to you. Ask Him to teach you from His Word every time you are about to read it.

- See the entire bible as the completely true book that it is.

- Have an open mind and a humble heart. Allow God to show you where you need to change.

- Look for applications in the bible that apply to your life and then line your life up with the Word. Use the bible as your standard of living.

- Think of the Word as God's love letter to you because He loves you so much!

- Listen to what God has to say to you through His Word, through your circumstances, through your prayers, and through the church.

- And finally, give yourself time. God wants to spend time with you. That's what relationships are all about!

The Word of God *is* living. It's active and sharp. It's penetrating and dividing, and it judges the thoughts and attitudes of your heart. Are you ready to become a sponge? Then soak up God's Word like my bible soaked up that bottle of water and you will never be the same again!

QUESTIONS TO PONDER

1. *How do you feel about God's Word? Is it alive or stale to you?*

2. *How has God shown you that He loves you in His Word? Do you see the Word as His love letter to you? Why or why not?*

3. *Do you listen to what God has to say to you through His Word?*

4. *Do you desire to spend time with God? Why do you think that is?*

5. *Is your personal relationship with God vibrant and growing? Why or why not?*

GOD'S WORD TO YOU

"Is not my word like fire," declares the LORD, "and like a hammer that breaks a rock in pieces?
Jeremiah 23:29

DAILY PRAYER

Dear Heavenly Father,
I ask that You would bring Your Word to life in a special way to me as I spend time with You. I also ask that You would teach me through Your Word so that I can know You more fully. Show me ways to apply Your Word to my life, and renew my mind. I thank You for Your inspired Word which is true. Open my ears to hear You and my eyes to see You. And change my heart to want what You want for me. In Jesus name I pray. Amen.

DAY 24

Out of Control!
By Lisa

It's nice when we have a day where everything goes the way we want it. The sun seems a little brighter and the colors seem more vivid. But many times, those days are few and far between.

Lately, I find that I feel a little out of control. But you know what? That's a good thing! It's not that I'm going crazy or anything, but more and more, I'm giving up control of my life and I'm giving it to God.

It's easy to focus on what's going wrong instead of what's going right, isn't it? As a Christian, God never promised us a rose garden. As a matter of fact, Jesus said we would be persecuted like He was. (John 15:20) Why is it then that when things don't go our way, we think it's not fair? Jesus *did* promise us His peace, a peace that surpasses understanding. (John 14:27, Philippians 4:7) We can find this peace in the midst of our trials. He also promised us His strength to go through the trials of life (Isaiah 41:10). Ultimately, God wants us to be out of control. Ok, maybe I should state that another way. God wants us to be out of the "control" business. He wants us to give Him control of our lives. The bible does say that we should have "self-control", but having self-control doesn't mean that we are in control of our lives. It means that we have given God control of our lives and we allow him to work through us. For you to live a life that is out of control is to submit to God and follow His will for your life. It all comes down to walking in step with the Spirit of God. Galatians 5:25 says, *"Since we live by the Spirit, let us keep in step with the Spirit."* When we can walk with the Spirit, we are truly giving God control. To walk with the Spirit means that we are in constant communion with God. It's also a lifestyle of obedience to the promptings of the Holy Spirit. If we aren't obedient to God, then we are lagging behind the Spirit. And when we come up with plans of our own without involving God, then we are walking ahead of the Spirit. But to walk *with* the Spirit means we hear God and obey Him immediately.

Walking with the Spirit is the same thing as living according to the Spirit. In Romans 8:5, the apostle Paul tells us how to live according to the Spirit. *"Those who live according to the sinful nature have their minds set on what that nature desires; but those who live in accordance with the Spirit have their minds set on what the Spirit desires."* So what has your mind been set on lately? Think about what a mindset is…. It's an inclination or a habit. Are you in the habit of talking to God daily? Are you in the habit of reading His word daily? Reading God's Word daily helps you to form your mindsets that guide your life and aids you in knowing God's will for your life. It's how you renew your mind.

So let's ask God to take control of every part of our life. The truth is, we don't really have control of as much of our lives as we'd like to think anyway. As we give Him control we will surely be in step with the Spirit, setting our minds on what the Spirit desires for us. Then you will be able to say with confidence that God is in control and you are *"out of control!"*

QUESTIONS TO PONDER

1. Are you in control of your life, or out of control?

2. What do you need to do to give God control of your life?

3. Do you have a specific area of your life that you try to control more than other areas? Which area is that?

4. What has your mind been set on lately?

5. Think about your life today. Are you walking with, lagging behind or running ahead of the Holy Spirit? What do you need to do to change this if you are not walking with the Spirit?

GOD'S WORD TO YOU

"The mind of sinful man is death, but the mind controlled by the Spirit is life and peace;"
Romans 8:6

DAILY PRAYER

Dear Heavenly Father,
I ask that You look into every part of my life and show me where I am not releasing control to You. I want to be out of control because I want You to be in control of my life. I want to walk in step with the Holy Spirit, setting my mind on the things that the Spirit desires. Thank You for removing old mindsets, and replacing them with the truth of Your Word. In Jesus name I pray. Amen.

DAY 25

It's Time to Surrender!
By Cindy

When someone says, *"I surrender!"* what do you normally think of? I usually think of someone waving a white flag and saying, *"I give up, you win!"* Or, if you are a long-time Christian like me, you usually think of someone accepting Jesus Christ as their personal Savior. Recently, I began to think about the term *surrender* in a totally different context.

For over 3 years now, Lisa and I have been praying and studying scripture together and at one time or other, one of us have said, "I just want to be emptied of myself and filled with the Holy Spirit so that when people hear me or read my words they can only say, "That's not Cindy or Lisa, that's God!" I know that we haven't gotten there yet and I can't say for sure if either of us will ever get there, but I do know that we want it more than anything! I've told Lisa many times that if we are going to talk the talk, we have to walk the walk. In order to do that, we know and understand that will require us to totally surrender every part of our lives to God!

I was listening to the new Third Day CD the other day and one of the songs is titled, *"Surrender."*[10] The song is about a lost person surrendering their life to Christ, but we can also look at these words for those of us that are already Christians. *"You better give up, gotta stop running. It's the end of the line, it's time to surrender. Hands up! Turn it around, fall to the ground, are you gonna surrender?"*[11] When was the last time you threw up your hands in surrender to the God of Heaven and then fell to the ground to say that you were sorry? We can't surrender everything, until we choose to give God everything. We must say, "God, I give up! I surrender! Here I am Lord, I die to myself. Empty me and fill me with your Holy Spirit! My life is Yours, use me!"

So what am I saying? We must surrender and give up control of our lives in order to be obedient and then we can live the abundant life that God intended for us since before He created the universe! I can hear you now, "Cindy, I would love to surrender everything to God and just read and study the Bible, but I have a job and a family that demands my attention!" And my response is, "Yes, you do!" But you can start small and give up that television show that you know is not of God and spend time getting to know God better. You can talk to your children about God and how we all will be held accountable for our actions. You can forget about social media for a week, you can make sure that you are not just a pew sitter, but an active participant in your church, you can......(fill in the blank). I know what I'm talking about because I kept telling Lisa about this television show that I just loved and finally I realized that I had to give it up because it was not of God.... Trust me, it has been very hard for me and especially now that the new season is on, it's really hard to pass this show up....but I do and you can too!

If you feel that your life is going nowhere fast, if you feel that you just keep praying and praying for the same thing over and over and God has not fulfilled the request, maybe it is time to take a closer and deeper look inside yourself. Have you surrendered your total life to Christ? Are your prayers given to God with a changed heart? Psalm 51:16-17 (The Message) makes that pretty clear: "*[16]Going through the motions doesn't please you; a flawless performance is nothing to you. [17]I learned God-worship when my pride was shattered. Heart-shattered lives ready for love doesn't for a moment escape God's notice.*"

QUESTIONS TO PONDER

1. Where God is concerned, are you just going through the motions?

2. What does it mean to you to totally surrender everything to God?

3. What can you give up today to show God that you surrender to Him?

4. Do you think it is possible to be obedient to God, yet not surrender to Him?

GOD'S WORD TO YOU

Then Jesus said to his disciples, "If anyone would come after me, he must deny himself and take up his cross and follow me. For whoever wants to save his life will lose it, but whoever loses his life for me will find it. What good will it be for a man if he gains the whole world, yet forfeits his soul? Or what can a man give in exchange for his soul?"
Matthew 16:24-26

DAILY PRAYER

*Dear Father God,
I am so amazed at how much You love me! Lord, I get so busy and caught up in my own life that I want to relinquish control and totally surrender my life to You. I want to be obedient and live each day for You, beginning right now, today, this very second! In your precious Son Jesus Christ's name I pray. Amen!*

DAY 26

Day By Day
By Cindy

If you walked into my study you would probably just shake your head, turn around and walk out. My walls are covered with large pieces of chart paper with my "To Do" lists on them. These are actually future plans and ideas that I am working on and don't want to forget. Taped to my walls are three months from a large desk calendar and I like to mark off each day with a large X.

The other day, I was sitting at my desk, looking at the calendars on my wall and looking ahead a couple of weeks to the day when my last school assignment is due. I had not removed the October calendar from my wall and all 31 of the big X's caught my eye. It suddenly dawned on me that those days were gone...*forever* and I would never get them back. Looking further into the future, I saw the plans that I had made for various activities and with the holidays fast approaching most of the days are already accounted for with something written in the little squares.

Looking at the future appointments, I was reminded of when I was young. I used to wish that I was old enough to drive, to graduate high school, to get married or something, and my mother would always say, *"You're just wishing your life away!"* Today, sitting here, looking at my calendar, I'm wondering if all of these future days that I have plans for is just wishing my life away. How about you? Are you wishing your life away?

We make all of our plans as if we are going to be here tomorrow, but James 4:15 says, *"Why, you do not even know what will happen tomorrow. What is your life? You are a mist that appears for a little while and then vanishes."* Jesus tells a parable of a rich man that is planning to build really big barns for his "bumper" crops and the rich man says to himself, *"If I work really hard right now and store up all of these provisions. Then I can rest because these things that I store up will last me for many years. After I've worked hard then I can eat, drink and be merry for the rest of my days!"* But, Jesus warns us in Luke 12:20, *"But God said to him, 'You fool! This very night your life will be demanded from you. Then who will get what you have prepared for yourself?"*

The Bible tells us that the only lasting treasure is the treasures that we build up in heaven. If your life was taken tonight, all your earthly treasures would be left behind.

Pastor Theodore Epp, founding director of *Back to the Bible Broadcast* said it best, *"Live your life as though Jesus Christ died yesterday, has been raised from the dead today and is coming again tomorrow."*[12] Living a life for Christ is the only way to store up heavenly treasures and it is the only way that you can be content when you see all the big X's marked off of your calendar.

QUESTIONS TO PONDER

1. Do you feel like you have been "wishing your life away?" If so how?

2. Have you consulted God for your future plans?

3. Is your mindset one of building up treasures in heaven or here on earth? What are you doing to build these treasures?

4. If your life were demanded of you tonight, who will get all that you've worked so hard for?

GOD'S WORD TO YOU

Do not store up for yourselves treasures on earth, where moth and rust destroy, and where thieves break in and steal. But store up for yourselves treasures in heaven, where moth and rust do not destroy, and where thieves do not break in and steal. For where your treasure is, there your heart will be also.
Matthew 6:19-21

DAILY PRAYER

Dear Father,
Thank You so much for creating me and giving me life. Lord, my prayer is that I will take this life and only use it for Your honor and glory, so that when others see me, they don't see me but they see You manifested in me. Lord, I pray that I will truly understand that what is most important are the treasures that I store up in heaven and not those that I work so hard to accumulate here on earth. Lord, I pray that You will give me the desire to learn more about Your Son, and the sacrifice that He made for me. In His precious name I pray, AMEN!

DAY 27

Basic Instructions for Life
By Cindy

The other day I passed a small church and on the marquee was written: *"BIBLE–Basic Instructions Before Leaving Earth"*. When I read this, I thought, "How clever." But then the more I thought about it I thought, "We are very fortunate because the Bible truly is an instruction manual that God so graciously gave to us!" You know, God didn't have to leave us a basic instruction manual....but He did. God didn't have to take the time to create this earth and everything on it so that we might have a nice place to live....but He did. God didn't have to plan for your birth and all the days of your life....but He did. When humans sinned, God didn't have to sacrifice His only Son so that we might be forgiven and have an eternal life with Him.....but He did.

So, let's look at these Basic Instructions Before Leaving Earth. God gave these instructions to us so that we might live a peaceful and content life while we have life here on earth. How often do we read these instructions? How often do we set aside time in our busy schedules to search these instructions to find out what it is that God wants us to know? The Basic Instructions Before Leaving Earth is "alive" and it speaks to each one of us in a personal way. Hebrews 4:12 says, *"For the word of God is living and active. Sharper than any double-edged sword, it penetrates even to dividing soul and spirit, joints and marrow; it judges the thoughts and attitudes of the heart."* If the Bible was important enough for God to write it, shouldn't it be important enough for us to read it? Especially if those instructions directly affect what is going to happen to us when we leave this earth? Shouldn't we be concerned enough with our eternity to read the manual?

One of these days, our lives on earth will end. I know, we don't like to think about that and we don't like to talk about it, but eventually we will have to deal with it. The Bible tells you straight up what will happen to you in eternity. Those who have accepted Jesus Christ as his/her personal Savior will spend eternity in Heaven, (I envision running up and down the golden streets) and those who have not accepted Jesus Christ as their Savior will spend eternity separated from God. Their destination is not Heaven, but will be Hell. The Basic Instructions Before Leaving Earth clearly covers that in detail. *"Listen to my instruction and be wise; do not ignore it. ^{34}Blessed is the man who listens to me, watching daily at my doors, waiting at my doorway. ^{35}For whoever finds me finds life and receives favor from the LORD. ^{36}But whoever fails to find me harms himself; all who hate me love death."* Proverbs 8:33-36

The Bible also gives us details of great men who tried desperately to be the best that they could be...but failed. The Bible tells us time and time again how God accepted their faults and still loved them. It also tells us how much God loves us, even though we fail him on a daily basis and how you and I sin against God daily, but he still loves us! The Bible tells us how we can never earn our salvation but it took Jesus Christ to willingly leave His throne in heaven to come and die a cruel death on the cross....just so you and I could enjoy an eternity of fellowship with God.

The Bible tells us about how we are not fighting flesh and blood but our fight is with Satan, who tries to make life miserable for us. Fortunately for us, the Bible also tells us that we can rest assured that because of the finished work of Christ on the cross, Satan and his minions have already been overcome. You and I are dealing with a defeated enemy! The cross of Christ has already defeated Satan *and* one day Christ will return to throw Satan and his minions into the Lake of Fire, never to be heard from again! Praise God!

God is good to us humans! He has planned every detail of our individual lives; He has given us an instruction manual that fills us in on the plans that He has for us. The only thing we have to do is read it! My question to you is, "If God cared enough for us that He would give us a detailed instruction manual on how to live life, then why is it so hard for some of us to read it?" It's not *just a book*. The Bible is alive and it is relevant to every situation in our lives today.

Think about setting aside some daily time to read *the only instruction manual* that has an eternal impact on you!

> *"Therefore, he who rejects this instruction does not reject man but God, who gives you his Holy Spirit."*
> —1 Thessalonians 4:8

QUESTIONS TO PONDER

1. Do you believe the Bible is God's Instruction manual to us? Why or why not?

2. Is your life peaceful and content? If not, do you think reading the Bible would help in that respect? Why or why not?

3. Is the Bible alive to you? How could a personal relationship with Jesus help with that?

4. How important is reading the "Basic Instructions Before Leaving Earth" to you? Does the time you spend in the Bible match up with your answer?

GOD'S WORD TO YOU

I will instruct you and teach you in the way you should go; I will counsel you and watch over you.
Psalm 32:8

All Scripture is God-breathed and is useful for teaching, rebuking, correcting and training in righteousness, ^{17}so that the man of God may be thoroughly equipped for every good work.
2 Timothy 3:16-17

DAILY PRAYER

Dear Father God,
Thank You so much, Lord, for giving me the Bible, Your Basic Instructions Before Leaving Earth, for my life and my eternity! Everything that I need to know about life, death, spiritual warfare and eternity is all in the instruction manual. Lord, You didn't have to leave me an instruction manual, but You did and it's because You love me so much and want me to have a great life while I'm living here on earth! Thank You! In your precious Son Jesus Christ's name I pray! Amen!

DAY 28

Making the Most of Your Time
By Lisa

Do you ever wish you could turn back the hands of time? When reflecting back over the year, it never seems to fail that there were some missed opportunities to share Jesus or share something you learned about God with someone else. But God tells us that we need to *"redeem the time"*.

> *"Walk in wisdom toward those who are outside, redeeming the time."*
> —Colossians 4:5 (NKJV)

> *"Be wise in the way you act toward outsiders; make the most of every opportunity."*
> —Colossians 4:5

When you study the Greek word for "redeem" in *The Complete Word Study Dictionary: New Testament* by Spiros Zodhiates,[13] it means to "buy back the time" or even, "to buy up all that is anywhere to be bought, and not allow the suitable moment to pass by unheeded but to make it one's own." What this tells us is that to redeem something is to free it at a price. Are you willing to redeem the time? If you are, it's going to cost you something. How can you make the most of every opportunity? You can invest your time, talents and resources into others.

Your life on earth is like a mist that is here one moment, and gone the next. You don't know if you will have another day, and you don't know if your friends or family will have another day. So it's really important to make the most of every opportunity.

> *"Now listen, you who say, "Today or tomorrow we will go to this or that city, spend a year there, carry on business and make money." Why, you do not even know what will happen tomorrow. What is your life? You are a mist that appears for a little while and then vanishes. Instead, you ought to say, "If it is the Lord's will, we will live and do this or that." As it is, you boast and brag. All such boasting is evil. Anyone, then, who knows the good he ought to do and doesn't do it, sins."*
> —James 4:13-17

How hard would it be to have a word of encouragement for someone who crosses your path? It would be making the most of that opportunity... How hard would it be to pray for someone who is lost or for someone who needs prayer? It would be making the most of your time... How hard would it be to give to others what God has so graciously given to you? Do you have money? Give money. Do you have food? Give food. Do you have wisdom? Teach others. Look at what God has given to you, and then give in return.

Don't look back and regret the time you've spent. Instead, look forward and redeem the time you have ahead of you! Make the most of every opportunity you have to share Christ and His love with others. It's going to require some forethought. Perhaps each morning you can ask, "What do I have to share about Jesus today?" Look at what you've learned from God's Word, and find something to share. Give someone encouragement, or hope, love, or compassion, mercy or grace, or any other number of attributes of God that you have learned from Him in His Word. Take some time to prepare yourself to help others by spending time alone with God. The more you spend time with Jesus, the more you will become like Him.

Are you willing to redeem the time for opportunities that will arise this week, this month, or even this year? Be prepared, because it will cost you! After a time, you can look back and know that you made the most of the opportunities that came your way, and you will see the joy that you gained from giving yourself to others!

QUESTIONS TO PONDER

1. *Have you been redeeming your time, or squandering your time?*

2. *What one thing can you change to start making the most of your time?*

3. *What have you been assuming you will be around for, when in reality, you don't know what God will allow you to do?*

4. *How can you best encourage those in your life? Think of a specific person who needs your encouragement.*

5. *What are you willing to give up in order to make the most of your time?*

GOD'S WORD TO YOU

Teach us to number our days aright, that we may gain a heart of wisdom.
Psalm 90:12

Be very careful, then, how you live—not as unwise but as wise, making the most of every opportunity, because the days are evil.
Ephesians 5:15-16

DAILY PRAYER

Dear Heavenly Father,
I admit that there are times when I squander my time and don't make the most of it. Lord, I ask You to forgive me. I want to make the most of my time by helping others. Help me to find those who need encouragement. And show me what I need to give up in order to make the most of my time. In Jesus name I pray. Amen.

DAY 29

Go Figure
By Cindy

I love to sit outside in the morning, drinking coffee and watching the world wake up. I always enjoy this time because this is when I feel the presence of God the most. The other morning, as I sat quietly listening to the birds singing, I thought to myself how they were praising God with their beautiful songs. As the morning sun began to creep over my flower bed, I saw the beautiful colors in the flowers and I could see the joy in their beauty as they lifted their petals toward heaven. Sitting at my feet were my two dogs. I call them my "posse" because they follow me wherever I lead them, unconditionally loving me and wanting only to have a relationship with me. I thought to myself, "Nature has it figured out, but we haven't."

We hurry about our daily lives as if we are "all that." We scurry from one project to another and most of the time we never think about God, let alone take time out of our busy schedules to *really* think about Him. In the first chapter of Genesis verse 26 God created man in His own image, in His own likeness. We are the pinnacle of God's creation! God, the Creator of the universe is our Father who *loves* us dearly and *wants* only to have a relationship with us....But, unfortunately, we who are God's ultimate creation have not figured it out.

Just think, before God created the universe, He already had you planned out in His mind. He knew exactly how you would look. He planned, to the tiniest detail, how you would look from the color of your hair, your eyes, and your skin. He planned your unique DNA and even your unique fingerprint! I still can't grasp the idea that no 2 people have the same fingerprints! God took the time to plan yours specifically.....to the tiniest detail. He decided who would be your parents, your siblings, when and where you would be born and even who the doctor would be that delivered you. I believe at that time, when you took your first deep breath and let out your first cry that God's eyes sparkled with a love for you that you could never fathom, because we are not capable of such deep love. You are the apple of God's eye....You and I are His ultimate creation, the ones that He is the most proud of!

Yet, why do we feel sometimes that we are alone? Why do we feel that if anything gets done we have to do it? Why do we allow ourselves to get so bogged down with daily activities that we forget what is truly important? Why do we get caught up in our own self-image? Why are we so concerned with how the world sees us? Why don't we just reach out and accept the rest, the comfort and the perfect peace that God is offering us through a total relationship with Him?

You are already the most beautiful creature in God's eyes, so why conform to society and what it says you should wear, what you should eat, or even how you should look? God's heart is so full of love that if we could feel His love for us, our feeble hearts would not be able to handle it.

What am I saying to you? You are beautiful just the way you are. You are God's perfect creation and all God wants from you is a relationship with Him. *Period!* When you get bogged down with everyday life or preferably before you allow yourself to get bogged down, take the time to worship God. Talk to Him and put God first in your life. Accept the loving relationship that He is offering you and then just spend time in His loving arms. When I feel that life is starting to overwhelm me, I ask God to put His arms around me and just hold me.....and you know what? *He does.* Let's open our eyes and truly see what God is offering us. Let's open up our hearts so that we truly worship our God and feel the love that He has for us. Let's open up our minds to prayer (a two way communication) with God and let Him help us, to finally figure it out!

QUESTIONS TO PONDER

1. What activities are you always scurrying from and to? Do you ever take the time to really think about God? Why or why not?

2. All of God's creation has figured it out. Have you?

3. Have you ever thought of yourself as the "Apple of God's eye?" Why or why not?

4. How does it make you feel to hear that God had you planned perfectly before He even created the universe?

GOD'S WORD TO YOU

Keep me as the apple of your eye; hide me in the shadow of your wings.
Psalms 17:8

DAILY PRAYER

Dear Father God,
Lord, I know that I often get bogged down with the busyness of life. Father! Help me to understand how much You love me. Help me to understand how much it means to You whether I get up in the morning or not. Lord, You are everything and I know that You thought about me even before you created me! Lord, help me to figure it all out. In Jesus name I pray! Amen!

DAY 30

Perfection and Excellence
By Lisa

I have to admit, I started writing this devotional today thinking that I would compare perfection versus excellence, as if they were independent of themselves. I had the whole thing written when I came upon the verse in 2 Corinthians 13:11, that says, *"...aim for perfection..."* What I found is that I need to *aim* for perfection *through* excellence while receiving grace to make mistakes. Let's face it…there was only one perfect man, and that was Jesus. And I know that perfection is unattainable, at least on this side of heaven. But we can and should work toward perfection, and that's where excellence comes in.

The definition of "excellence" is to outdo or surpass, but we can walk in excellence as we move toward perfection. What else does God say about what we should do for Him? In Colossians 3:17, we're told *"And whatever you do, whether in word or deed, do it all in the name of the Lord Jesus, giving thanks to God the Father through Him."* Also, 1 Corinthians 10:31 states, *"So whether you eat or drink or whatever you do, do it all for the glory of God."* Isn't that our ultimate purpose…to do all that we do in such a way that it brings the most glory to God? That sounds like "excellence" to me. God wants us to do things in such a way that if Jesus Himself was the recipient of our act of service, it would be pleasing to Him and would honor God. Well, in a way, Jesus is the recipient of all of our acts of service. Remember what Jesus said, *"...whatever you did for one of the least of these brothers of mine, you did for me".* (Matthew 25:40) When we think of Jesus as being the recipient of those things that we'd rather not do, we'll be more likely to treat others with the love of Jesus. And we can't help but excel, or do things with "excellence" the more we love like Jesus loves.

Think about the clothes you buy. Have you ever seen the little quality control sticker that shows that the item you purchased passed a quality control inspection? Well, think about stamping your acts of service with "Approved by JESUS" on everything you do that glorifies God. Did you act in a loving way? Stamp it "Approved by JESUS". Did you help out a friend in need? Stamp it "Approved by JESUS". Or, did you berate your coworker on the phone or even in your head? You know God will send that back for a do-over and have you try again until you can stamp it with, "Approved by JESUS"!

We will always fail when perfection is demanded, but we can move toward perfection as we walk out our lives in excellence. And when we give ourselves and others the grace to make mistakes and learn from them we can move into new areas of excellence. Let's work with excellence and aim toward perfection. The Holy Spirit will help us to continually do better and better in all areas of our lives as we are willing to yield to Him.

QUESTIONS TO PONDER

1. *Do you ever think of the things you'd rather not do as doing them for Jesus? How might that make them easier to do?*

2. *Do you aim for perfection or excellence in the things you do for God?*

3. *Why is it so much easier to do loving things for Jesus than for someone else?*

4. *Do you know that God doesn't expect perfection from you, but offers grace when you make mistakes? When have you seen this?*

GOD'S WORD TO YOU

And whatever you do, whether in word or deed, do it all in the name of the Lord Jesus, giving thanks to God the Father through him.
Colossians 3:17

DAILY PRAYER

Dear Heavenly Father,
I know that there was only one perfect man, and that is Your Son, Jesus. I thank You for giving me the grace to become more and more like Him. I thank You that I don't have to be perfect because only You are perfect. And thank You for showing me how to give grace to others. Help me on my walk toward perfection through excellence. In Jesus name I pray. Amen.

APPENDIX A

Becoming a Believer

With all of the trees blooming and flowers budding, spring is a beautiful display of new life. Just like a flower goes through a process from a dead seed that's growing into a flower with full blooms, receiving the new life of Christ is also a process. For those of you who are interested in becoming a Christian, here are some points to guide you in the most important decision you'll ever make in your life – becoming a follower of Christ.

First, *admit* to yourself and to God that you have sinned. **Romans 3:23** tells us *"…for all have sinned and fall short of the glory of God"*. Sin is what separates you from God, who is holy. Truly understanding this separation from God brings about a godly sorrow that leads you to repent from your sins, or to turn away from your sin and turn to God. Confess your sins to God and receive His forgiveness for all your sins, past, present and future. **2 Corinthians 7:10** *"Godly sorrow brings repentance that leads to salvation and leaves no regret, but worldly sorrow brings death."* **Acts 3:19** *"Repent then, and turn to God, so that your sins may be wiped out, that times of refreshing may come from the Lord"*.

Believe in Jesus' sacrifice on the cross and His resurrection. Did you know that Jesus, who was the only perfect man, took the sins of the world and our punishment for those sins so that you could be right with God? He also rose from the dead and is seated at the right hand of God in heaven. In **John 5:24**, Jesus said, *"I tell you the truth, whoever hears my word and believes Him who sent me has eternal life and will not be condemned; he has crossed over from death to life."*

Confess your belief in Jesus. **Romans 10:9** tells us *"That if you confess with your mouth, 'Jesus is Lord,' and believe in your heart that God raised Him from the dead, you will be saved."*

Then realize that the forgiveness and eternal life that God has for you is a free gift that you must receive for yourself. **Ephesians 2:8-9** *"For it is by grace you have been saved, through faith – and this is not of yourselves, it is the gift of God – not by works, so that no one can boast."*

As you continue with the process and are ***baptized*** by immersion, just like Jesus was, you are sharing in Jesus' death and resurrection by showing that you are dying to your old ways as you go under the water, and you are raised to your new life in Christ as you come up from the watery grave!

Jesus promises eternal life for those who believe in Him. In **John 3:16** He said, ***"For God so loved the world that He gave His one and only Son, that whoever believes in Him shall not perish but have eternal life."***

Your new life in Christ is all about a ***personal relationship*** with Jesus. It's listening and learning in addition to asking; it's praising God and giving thanks to Him in all situations; it's serving Him and obeying Him in whatever way He asks. With new life comes growth. And you do this by finding a bible-based church with other loving Christians who can become your church family and help you to grow in the Word of God and in the fruit of the Spirit. As you accept Christ, know that you have an enemy, the devil, who will try to keep you separated from God and your church family.

If you find Jesus tugging at your heart, telling you it's time to know Him personally, pray to God and let Him know that you have sinned and you need a Savior. Let Him know that you want Him to be the Lord of your life as you begin your walk to know Him personally. Pray your own prayer, or pray something like the following:

Dear Heavenly Father,
I know I have sinned and need Jesus as my Savior. I believe Jesus paid for my sins and was raised to life from the dead. I ask You to be the Lord of my life. In Jesus name I pray. Amen.

Know that as you have accepted Jesus as your Lord and Savior, God has welcomed you into His kingdom for eternity and has sealed you with the Holy Spirit. Be assured that you are a child of God even if you don't feel any different. And understand that knowing Jesus personally is a walk you'll continue on for the rest of this life and into eternity.

REFERENCES

1. Brandon Heath CD: *What If We*, Released July 2008, song referenced from the CD: Give Me Your Eyes

2. "Give Me Your Eyes" lyrics - http://www.elyrics.net/read/b/brandon-heath-lyrics/give-me-your-eyes-lyrics.html

3. Hogan's Heroes: http://www.imdb.com/title/tt0058812/

4. Horatio G. Spafford story: http://voices.yahoo.com/horatio-g-spafford-story-behind-hymn-is-1620793.html

5. "It Is Well with My Soul" lyrics: http://www.hymnsite.com/lyrics/umh377.sht

6. "Christ the Solid Rock" lyrics Reference: "On Christ the Solid Rock" written by Edward Mote 1797-1874

7. The Chronicles of Narnia by C.S. Lewis published between October 1950 and March 1956, published by McMillan.

8. Third Day CD: *MOVE*, Released October 19, 2010, song referenced from the CD: Lift Up Your Face

9. Abraham Lincoln quote: Reference: Abraham Lincoln quote http://www.quotationspage.com/quote/27074.html

10. Third Day CD: MOVE, Released October 19, 2010, song referenced from the CD: Surrender

11. Surrender lyrics: http://thirdday.com/songs/surrender

12. Theodore Epp quote:
    http://www.preach-the-gospel.com/Theodore-Epp-Quotes.htm

13. Spiros Zodiates:
    http://www.amginternational.org/www/docs/10421.4882/heritage-history-zodhiates

A WORD FROM LVC MINISTRIES

We hope that you have enjoyed reading these daily devotionals as much as we have enjoyed writing them. Lisa and I are amazed how God has used us to write for Him. In the beginning when we started to write weekly devotionals we would say to each other, "I think I will write about this…." We found out really quickly that God had other plans as He always directed us to write about something completely different than what we thought we would write about. Writing devotionals has been a part of our growing period with God and we are looking forward to being obedient and following His will wherever He leads us!

We know the plans that God has for us. As a Christian, the most important thing that you can do is wait upon the Lord in order for Him to grow you and strengthen you into the son or daughter that He intends for you to be. Even though you might know the plans that God has for you, it is very important that you wait for the Lord to grow you and to clear the path ahead of you so that you will run the race that He has planned for you!

To continue following LVC Ministries on the web, please go to www.LVCMinistries.com. Like us on facebook at www.facebook.com\LVCMinistries.

ABOUT THE AUTHORS

*C*indy Cross lives in Fort Worth, Texas with her husband Ronnie and their two dogs. She holds a Bachelor of Science degree in Business Administration from Florida Southern College in Lakeland, Florida and also a Master of Education degree in Teaching from The University of Texas at Arlington. For many years, she has been actively involved with the mentor-mentee programs and Women's Ministries from various churches. Cindy feels that her ministry is to teach, write and minister to women of all ages. She has been a member of Southwest Christian Church for over five years.

Lisa Vanderbilt lives in Fort Worth, Texas with her husband, Kirk. She is a proud mother to her son, Scott and her daughter, Tara. Lisa holds a Bachelor of Business Administration degree in Business Analysis from Texas A&M University in College Station, Texas. She has spent time in leadership as a Children's Leader and a Group Leader in Bible Study Fellowship (BSF). Lisa has been a part of Southwest Christian Church for over 20 years and a part of their Worship Team over 10 years. Her passion is to study God's Word, and to motivate others by teaching God's Word through her speaking and writing.

CPSIA information can be obtained
at www.ICGtesting.com
Printed in the USA
FFOW01n1737291013
2216FF

9 781936 746514